TURNING POINTS

by MARTHA SMOCK

Unity Books
Unity Village, Missouri 64065

Turning Points was first published in 1976.
Revised edition 1985

Cover photograph by
Todd Powell

Contents

Introduction

This is a book about turning points.

I know that you can look back on your life and say about some experience, ''That was the turning point!''

Always we think of a turning point as sort of an about-face. Where everything looked black, suddenly light came. Where life hung in the balance, the turning point came, the crisis passed, healing took place.

Where there seemed to be no way to meet some situation, an idea came, help was unexpectedly offered, solutions appeared—it was a turning point!

It was as though we got on an elevator marked *Down* and went *Up* instead. It was as though we had already settled for failure, when suddenly someone acclaimed us a winner. It was as though we had awakened from a dream to find that it was not a dream after all but a wonderful reality!

Turning points. These must be God's delightful road signs that say:

"This way to health."

"This way to happiness."

"This way to peace of mind."

"This way to fulfillment and success."

If this book can help you recognize turning points in your life, I will be grateful.

If this book can help you come consciously to turning points rather than flounder in doubt and darkness, I will be grateful.

If this book can in any way be a turning point for you in your thinking, I will be grateful.

Martha Smock
1976

No Need to Wait

You know, you do not have to wait for a turning point. You can make your own!

We should not sit around hoping for a change, a break, for something to happen. We have it in our power to turn that corner, to make the change, to start things going in a different direction.

We should never think that we are too old to make a change, that it is too late to begin again. We do not have to go along with unhappy conditions or accept ill-health, lack, and limitation as our lot. The turning point comes first of all *in us,* in some outer circumstance.

Prayer is a turning point.

We talk a great deal about turning within in prayer. Affirmative prayer is really just that—a turning about of our inner thoughts and feelings, a turning about of our habitual reactions to life.

Prayer is turning within, turning away from negative thinking, turning our thoughts toward light and Truth.

We have all made these inner turnings in prayer and meditation, and we know how they have wrought wonderful changes in us and in the conditions of our lives.

When we think about the turning points of our lives we can see that sometimes they came about in most unexpected ways.

Sometimes the turning point was a welcome change; sometimes we have had change thrust upon us that we fought or rebelled against. But it proved to be a turning point for good, a turning point in the right direction, after all.

I believe that we can consciously decide to make a turning point in our lives. I also believe that unconsciously, without being aware of it, we bring ourselves to turning points.

I do not believe that we ever come to a turning point totally unprepared. We are ready for it. In our spiritual selves, we have chosen it.

I also believe that the most important turning points we make are the turning points that have to do with our consciousness of God, of ourselves as spiritual beings, with our realization of our oneness with our very Source. These are the greatest turning points of all!

In the following chapters we will consider some turning points that can lead to a happier, freer, healthier, more successful life.

I

Turning Points in Healing

You Can Be Healed

I do not pretend to know all there is to know about healing, but I do know what I have learned about healing in my own experience. And from my many years of association with Silent Unity I have come to a firm belief that every condition can be healed, that truly, with God all things are possible.

It is easy to believe in healing, to accept the idea of health as right and natural, when one feels well and strong, which is the way most of us feel most of the time.

It is when illness strikes us or someone dear to us that our faith is put to the test. Perhaps we have, as far as we know, always thought in positive terms, in terms of health and wholeness. We may find ourselves say, as I did when some years back I was meeting a severe health challenge, "But I've never been sick a day in my life!"

It finally dawned on me that this was not important. It was like a drowning man saying, "But I've never drowned in my life!" The need was to do something, to rise out of the condition, to find healing, just as the person who thinks he is drowning has to float, or find something to hang on to, or in some way extricate himself from the water.

Myrtle Fillmore said that she had had a physical condition that did not seem to respond to prayers or faith, no matter how persistent she was. She said that as she was praying for light, it came to her: *You have searched among your faults, now search among your virtues.*

Those of us who are trying to live by Truth teachings, trying to keep our thinking positive and constructive, trying to express only ideas of life and goodness are likely to wonder, when we become ill, where we have failed, where we have gone wrong. We search our consciousness for faults and failings.

Myrtle Fillmore said that when it came to her that she was to search among her virtues, she realized that she had prided herself on keeping everything bottled up within herself. She could see that she had mistaken suffering in silence for patience and forbearance.

As she was able to let go inner feelings of frustration and let the joy and freedom of Spirit take over in her and express through her, she was healed.

Some of us may, without realizing it, have a sort of false pride about our need for healing. I discovered that I did. It took my ten-year-old daughter to help me see this. I did not want to admit that I needed healing, needed help; I did not want anyone outside the family to know that I had any such need. This child quite calmly said to me one day, "You know, Mother, you are not God." Like Myrtle Fillmore, I needed to search among my virtues, or what I thought of as virtues, which was never to admit even to myself (much less to anyone else) that I was less than perfectly healthy. This then was part of my healing.

Many times people ask for prayers for healing from Silent Unity, and when they are not healed, they may ask Silent Unity to tell them why. Silent Unity never attempts to do this, for no one can know another's inmost feelings or inmost soul. But Silent Unity always prays for the healing of the whole person. Healing is, of course, healing of the body; but spiritual healing includes healing of the emotions, healing of the thoughts and feelings.

One friend said that when she was a young woman, she wrote to Silent Unity for healing prayers, at the suggestion of a relative. When she was not healed, she wrote again, wanting to know what she was doing wrong. She said that Silent Unity told her to search her consciousness to see if there was anything she was harboring that she needed to let go.

She had a stepfather whom she had hated since she was twelve years old. She took up the idea of forgiveness, and instead of praying for healing alone, she prayed for the forgiving love of Christ to help her overcome her feelings of resentment and hatred. She said that before long the stepfather told her mother that he had never seen such a change in anyone as in this girl. She was writing us fifty years later to tell us about it, and said that she had never had to have the operation that the doctors said was absolutely necessary at the time. Her healing came through forgiveness.

Sometimes, many times, the need for healing is linked with the need for forgiveness. We may have been holding unforgiving thoughts about others. More times than not, we are unforgiving of ourselves. We keep some unhappy incident of the past alive by continually bringing it to mind. We feel that we cannot be forgiven. A woman said that not until she was eighty years of age did she finally realize what forgiveness meant. Now she was able to see herself in a new light. She felt free for the first time of the burden of guilt she had been carrying.

It is always a good idea to practice forgiveness. Charles Fillmore calls forgiveness "the sure remedy for every ill the flesh is heir to." He suggests that one mentally forgive everyone and everything—even an animal—that he has felt any antipathy toward, before going to bed at night. To do this is to clear away negation from our minds and hearts and to make us open and receptive channels for God's healing, harmonizing love.

What do we do? How do we handle feelings of fear that come when we or those dear to us are faced with conditions that are termed incurable?

In my own experience, at one time the verdict was that I could not expect to be healed. This was the clear realization that came to me, "Not my will, not the doctor's will, but Thy will be done." I was willing to utterly release myself to God, to His will, and healing came.

When we realize that God's will is always life and healing, that God's will is always good, we can make this utter commitment to His will.

One of the most helpful healing articles we published in *DAILY WORD* was written around this idea. It was the story of Sallman, who painted the famous head of Christ portrait. He had been given a negative prognosis by his doctor and was told to set his affairs in order. But when he told his wife and they prayed, it was not for healing alone. Their prayer was, "Not my will but thine be done." Sallman prayed to be shown what he was to do with his life, how he could make his life meaningful. His healing came, and he was inspired to paint the picture of Christ that became famous.

Many times in praying for healing, we become discouraged; we give up too easily. We accept what someone else says about our condition, or we may even allow ourselves to fall into thinking of ourselves as weak or helpless. We let the body dictate to us, rather than lifting up the body though faith.

The body is intelligent; it responds to our word of truth, it responds to our prayers. But the great realization that comes to us in praying for healing is that healing has to come from within ourselves, that it is more than a matter of just the right healing words, more than a matter of believing in

God's power to heal. It is a matter of actually laying hold of the life idea, of incorporating it into our very being. How do we do this? Affirmations are wonderfully helpful, for they turn us away from thinking in terms of disease or illness. But the affirmation has to become more than words thought about or even spoken aloud. The affirmation must become a feeling that pervades not just our thought but our whole being. Are we affirming life? Then we have to feel life in every part of us. *". . . Then from my flesh I shall see God . . . ."* (Job 19:26) We need to let the life idea take over in our very flesh.

The call to life is being sounded continually in us. At the time I was experiencing my health challenge, I was in a hospital. It had been a time of walking through the valley of the shadow for me, a time when my mind affirmed and tried to stay with all the Truth that I knew; but still my body did not respond.

I remember vividly two dreams I had at that time. In one dream it was as though I had awakened, and I felt small and helpless lying there in the hospital bed. A voice somewhere above me said, "This is not all of you." I answered, "Yes, it is." And the voice said again, "This is not all of you.'' The other dream was of myself spinning in space. I was a globe, I was a sphere saying, ''It's all in you. It's all in you.''

I thought a great deal about these dreams and their meaning, and I knew they were bringing me a message of life, calling me back to life.

When we have to deal with a physical problem, it sometimes seems that the body is all-important. All attention is given to the body, its functioning, its temperature, its day-to-day response to treatment, and so on. And in working so hard to heal the body, we may overlook the Healer.

''This is not all of you'' was to remind me that I was more than flesh and blood—I was Spirit. The dream about the globe must have been to remind me that my life was without beginning or end. The words, ''It's all in you,'' were to remind me that the healing I was seeking, the understanding I was seeking about the experience in which I found myself, the light that I was groping for—all these were already in me: the Truth was in me, God was in me, the answers I was seeking were in me.

I had been praying for healing; I had been affirming life, strength, and health. Now I held to these words, to this idea: *I am the resurrection and the life.*

All of us, when going through experiences that demand all our faith, that challenge everything in us, search for new clues to Truth and healing, new light on this matter of life.

"This is not all of you." Was the inner Christ telling me in a vision, in a dream: "Seek Me, find Me, know Me. I am your life. I am the resurrection and the life"?

"It's all in you." Was this same Spirit in me saying to me: "Why look outside yourself? Here I am, the Spirit of life, mighty in the midst of you. All that you need, all that you will ever need is encompassed in Me. Your life is hid with Me in God"?

The words "Be still, and know that I am God" were especially helpful to me in quieting my fears, in harmonizing my emotions, in becoming outwardly and inwardly still. This may not sound like a healing prayer, but it is: *Be still, and know that I am God.*

Then follow this feeling of deep inner quietness, this feeling of the presence of God, with the realization that your body is the temple of the living God. *Do you not know that your body is a temple of the Holy Spirit within you, which you have from God? . . . So glorify God in your body.* (I Cor. 6:19-20)

I remember saying this over and over to myself at a time when I really needed to realize it. I thought about the words "glorify God in your body," and to me they meant, "Show forth God's healing in your body." This is your way of glorifying God. You are to shine with health, you are to glow with health, you are to be a radiant, living expression of health.

An affirmation that has been especially helpful to me is: *There is only one life, God-life. This life flows freely through me from the top of my head to the soles of my feet, cleansing, purifying, renewing, healing, and restoring me.*

Miracles of healing are taking place every day. Negative verdicts are being pronounced all the time. This is what we should remember, rather than allowing ourselves to think of all the negative statistics. If even one person can be healed, so can anyone.

If you need healing, you can be healed. This is what you are to believe and to have faith in. It is the truth. You can be healed. God's will for you is life and healing.

And with God all things are possible. Where is God? God is in the midst of you. God is right where you are. God is the life within you. God is saying to you now: "You are My beloved child. I am your life, I am mighty in the midst of you. Your faith has made you whole. Go your way in peace."

Strength for Your Days

There are times in our lives when we feel that we are not strong enough to meet some situation, but there is never a time when we do not have available to us all the strength, all the help, all the power we need to meet anything, to rise above and out of any situation or condition.

God gives us strength for our days, and He gives us the strength we need at the time we need it. He gives us the kind of help, the kind of strength that seems to be our present or particular need.

Should we awaken in the morning feeling weak or lifeless, let our first thought be: *God is my strength. God is my life.*

Feelings of weakness are overcome by affirming strength, by taking our stand with God, by holding to and relying on His strong Spirit within us.

Everything in us responds to our word of

strength. When we say with conviction and faith: *I am strong in the Lord, and in the power of His might,* the words take on life and power. We do not just say them, we feel them. We feel strengthened and renewed; we feel a response in every part of our body. The cells seem to sing a song of renewal and rejoicing.

We do not need ever to give in to weakness. We do not need ever to feel that we do not have strength, for God is with us. He is our life, He is our strength; it is He who upholds us, who heals us, who fills us with strong and vitalizing life.

Many times, though we are strong and well physically, we lack emotional strength. We find ourselves easily upset, easily disturbed. We are sensitive and quick to tears, and we long to be strong and calm.

God is the strength of our hearts, of our emotional nature, even as He is the strength of our bodies. We can turn to God for the strength we need, and He will not fail to give it to us.

Instead of thinking of ourselves as easily upset, as quick to go to pieces, let us change this thought; let us give our minds and hearts a new thought, a new outlook, a new attitude. Let us say to ourselves: *I am strong in the Lord. In Him I am calm, poised, radiant, confident.* God in us is our strength, the kind of strength we need, the kind of strength we long for. We can be, *we are,* strong in the Lord and in the power of His might.

God is our strength. His is the Spirit in us that keeps us keeping on. It is well to remember Paul's words: *I can do all things in him who strengthens me,* (Phil. 4:13) to use these words for ourselves, to remind ourselves that through the power of God in us, the Christ in us, we can do all things. We can accomplish that which we set out to do. We can make the contribution to life, to God, to man, that we long in our hearts to make. God in us keeps us going. God in us strengthens us in will and purpose. God in us says: ''Never give up. I am with you. I am your strength.''

The kind of strength we need, the kind of strength that is the answer to every need, is spiritual strength, which we already have if we but knew it and realized it.

We need to remember that we are essentially spiritual beings, that when God made us we were first of all spiritual creations, made in His image and likeness, having His powers inherent in us.

It may seem to us that we are not very strong in things of the Spirit, that we do not have much understanding, that we are lacking in faith. But there are depths of the Spirit in us that we have not yet discovered. There is inherent faith within us that we have not yet tested or used.

There is spiritual power in us, for God has put His Spirit in us. Just as we do not want to let thoughts of physical or emotional weakness stay with us, so we do not want to continue to think of ourselves as lacking spiritual strength. We believe this only if we forget where our strength comes from, Who it is that lives in us, moves through us, gives us life and breath and being. Everything in us rises up in strength, in faith, in power, when we realize the unity, the oneness that we have with God.

"As your days, so shall your strength be." God gives you strength for every day. He gives you the kind of strength you need, at the time you need it.

God is the strength of your body. In Him you are vitalized; through Him you are healed. God is the strength of your emotions. In Him you are kept poised and serene; through Him you are blessed.

God is the strength of your will and purpose. In Him you are kept steady and strong; through Him you achieve and accomplish.

God is the strength of your spirit. In Him you

find light; through Him you gain grace and glory.

Learn to Say No

A woman who was finding her way back to health after a long siege of both physical and mental stress said that one of the most important things she gained through the experience was the ability to say *no*.

This seems contradictory if healing is a result of affirmation, of saying *yes* to life. But to say *no* can be a positive act, it can be a part of healing.

To learn to say *no* to the unnecessary, the trivial, is to make room in your life for the meaningful, the larger things of Spirit.

The place where saying *no* is most important is in your own mind. What you deny is as necessary to healing as what you affirm.

The woman who sensed that she had made real progress because she could say *no* to many of the things that came crowding in to demand her time and attention had taken a larger step than she knew. Where before she had been fearful and unsure of herself, afraid of what others might think of

her, now she was gaining inner calmness and peace
and an awareness of herself as a child of God. She
was no longer afraid to take command, no longer
afraid to follow her inner light and leading.

Most persons do not realize how many false
beliefs they cling to, how many fears they carry
with them. They believe something because everyone else does. They may not find it easy to change
the old ways of thinking.

No matter how long you have believed in some
negative proposition, your belief still does not
make it true. The fact that for centuries people
believed the world to be flat did not make it true.

You can say *no* firmly and fearlessly to any belief
in anything less than God, to any belief that there
can be any presence or power other than God, the
good omnipotent. You can say *no* to negation in
any form by withdrawing your belief in it, by saying in effect: "You are nothing. You have no
power."

Negation is like darkness. You do not have to
battle it, you do not have to beg it to be gone; you
only have to turn on a light to vanquish it.

Affirmations turn on the light. The light of God
is always at hand for you. It streams in upon you as
you turn from the darkness, as you know and feel

your oneness with God.

If you have some need or problem, think about it simply in terms of *yes* and *no*.

If you have a health need, ask yourself what you are saying *yes* to, what you are saying *no* to. Sometimes when we do this, we are startled to find that we have actually been saying *no* to the positive and *yes* to the negative.

How would you answer these questions?

Do you believe that there is any condition impossible of healing?

Do you believe that God's will is that you experience difficulty and suffering?

Do you believe that age and other conditions can retard healing?

Do you believe that you can inherit disease?

The positive way to answer *no* to such beliefs, to deny them effectively and completely, is to answer in the form of an affirmation such as the following:

I believe that with God all things are possible. His life is the only life, His power is the only power, and this life and power are mighty in the midst of me to heal, to renew, to perfect, to restore.

God's will for me is good and only good.

Healing is from God and is not affected by time or space, age, or any other condition. In God, I am

ageless, deathless, one with God's eternal life.
I inherit only life and health and wholeness from
God, my Father.

Can you agree with these affirmations? Can you
say *yes* to them? To do so is to lift up your thought,
to enter a new area of spiritual awareness, to think
of yourself in terms of spiritual life, to put yourself
on the side of life.

The Life of God—
Above, Beneath, Within You

"In the life of Omnipresence do I dwell,
    'Tis above, around, within me, all is well;
    Life divine forever guiding all my ways,
    Life divine forever filling all my days."

You live in God; you dwell in the life of omnipresence. You are never apart from God; you are
never apart from His presence; you are never separated from His love.

The life of God is strong and powerful within
you. It flows through you, a mighty healing
stream. God's life within you is pure, perfect, indestructible; it is endless and eternal. Relax and

rest in the realization that you live in God, that you are sustained and healed by His life. Know that there is nothing to fear, for God is with you. His life surrounds and enfolds you; it is above, around, within you, and all is well.

"In the love of Omnipresence do I rest,
   Feel it filling, thrilling through me, blessed
         guest!
   Love divine all discord soothing into peace,
   Love divine in whose sweet presence pain
         doth cease."

Rest in the love of God, relax in the love of God, trust in the love of God. The love of God fills your mind and heart, bringing you peace and perfect freedom. There is nothing to fear, for God is with you; His love is poured out upon you. There is only harmony in God; His love soothes, sustains, and comforts you.

The tranquilizing power of divine love eases all tension and brings release from pain. You rest in the love of God. You are healed and restored now by the healing love of God, strong and perfect within you.

"In the Truth of Omnipresence do I stand,
   For the power of the Almighty holds my
         hand.

> Truth divine, supreme, unchanging, all art
>   thou!
> Truth divine, thy word is freedom, spoken
>   now.''

Where do you stand? Wherever you are right now, you stand in the Truth of God. ''. . . *The place on which you are standing is holy ground.''* (Exod. 3:5) The holy ground is your faith and your consciousness of Truth. As you stand strong in this consciousness, as you know and believe that through all things, through all experiences, through all situations, there is only God, that only His good prevails, you stand strong, unshakable, immovable.

God is the only power. Knowing this you have no fear; knowing this you are serene, calm, poised, and trusting. Knowing this you meet each day with the assurance that you are not alone, that the power of the Almighty holds your hand.

> ''Life and love and Truth, forever Thou art
>   mine!
> Glorious trinity of heaven, all divine,
> Oh, my soul doth sing with rapture hymns
>   of praise,
> And my feet shall walk with gladness in thy
>   ways.''

In the life of Omnipresence you dwell, in the love of Omnipresence you rest, in the Truth of Omnipresence you stand. Hold to this assurance, live in it, find renewal in it. Then all the outer happenings will assume their rightful proportions; you will not be overcome by appearances.

There is never any condition that is beyond God's power to heal. Right now you live in God. His life lives through you. There is never any inharmony beyond the power of God's love to transform and bless. Right now the love of God surrounds you, enfolds you; you are filled with the love of God, and this love finds perfect expression in and through you.

II

Turning Points We Sometimes Resist

It Is Not the End of the World

It is not the end of the world! It may be the end of a job. It may be the end of a relationship. It may be the end of a marriage. It may be the end of a way of life. But it is not the end of the world.

Sometimes shattering experiences come. Things happen that are unexpected and difficult to accept. For the moment, we may feel forsaken and lost; we may feel like giving up, giving in to the rush of fear and negative emotions that sweep over us.

But even in the most dire circumstances, even at those times when our way is dark and depressing, the darkness will pass. There is a light shining, and it is shining in us! Life holds much that is wonderful for us. This may be hard for us to believe, but we will find it to be true, as have countless other persons who have been faced with all kinds of situations and have come through them. We can too!

Life is a passing scene, but the truth of our being endures through all the comings and goings, through all the changes, expected and unexpected. What does this mean? The truth of our being is that we are more than we seem, more than we have believed ourselves to be, more than we have yet expressed. Something in us knows this; something in us is unconquerable even in defeat. This is God's own Spirit in us, the Christ in us, the Self of us which is undaunted, fearless, free.

Whatever may cause us to feel rejected, unloved, unworthy, whatever may cause us to feel afraid, whatever may cause us to feel bitter or hurt, whatever may cause us to feel like a failure—we can let it go. It has no power. Christ in us is greater. This too shall pass. The truth of our being remains.

How can we pick up the pieces? What can we do? The place to begin is not with the outer condition or circumstance but with ourselves, with our inner feelings, with our thoughts. We need to listen not to the voice of despair or defeat but to the inner Spirit that speaks the truth to us. If we have been desperately praying for God to help us, it is time now to be still, to be as still as we possibly can be, to turn ourselves and all that concerns us over to God, the power, the presence that is always with us.

"Be still, and know that I am God." Be still, troubled thoughts. Be still, anxious feelings. Be still, self-accusations. Be still, fearful imaginings. Be still. Be still. Be still, and know that I am God.

Though we do not see our way, there is a way. God will show us the way. Be still, and know that I am God.

Though we do not feel that we can face life, we can. With God's help we can begin again. Be still, and know that I am God.

Though we may feel that all is lost, this is not true. With God all things are possible, and God is with us. Be still, and know that I am God.

There is a resurrecting Spirit in you, a Spirit that reminds you that life is unlimited, eternal. This is the message to you from your Christ indwelling: "I am the resurrection and the life. I am your resurrection and your life. I am the overcoming power in you. I am the life of your being. I am the strength of your spirit. I am the support of your soul. I am the fulfillment of your highest hopes. I am the infinite possibility in you."

Does it seem like the end of the world? It may be

the end of something that has been a part of your experience, an important and vital part, perhaps— but only a part. Though you may not be able to see the whys and wherefores of what seems to you now to be a devastating experience, eventually you will come to see and know that even this takes its place as only a passing part of the overall pattern of good that is your life as a spiritual being.

You are needed, you are important, you are worthy, you have your own place to fill in this world. You are God's own child in whom He has placed the resurrecting, overcoming Spirit of the Christ.

When Is Your Birthday?

Many persons dread the thought of birthdays, for to them a birthday is only another sign of the rapid passage of time.

But no one need ever feel this way on his or her birthday. With birthdays, as with everything else in life, the event itself is not important, but our thought about it is. There is a way to think about birthdays that banishes the fear of age, that emphasizes the spiritual importance of birthdays.

When is your birthday? It is whenever you make a new beginning in your life; it is whenever new understanding dawns in you; it is whenever you strive to become a better person.

When is your birthday? It is when you discover Truth for yourself, when you realize that you are a spiritual being. Such a thought about birthdays has nothing to do with the passing of time. The progress of Spirit is not measured in terms of time as we know it but by the breadth and depth of our understanding, our faith, our power to love.

When did you really begin to live? Not on the day you were born, not on your twenty-first birthday, not on your fortieth birthday. You really began to live when you first became aware of yourself as a living soul sent forth from God; when you first became aware of the mystical but wonderful bond that exists between you and all other persons, between you and God. You first began to live when the ''Word became flesh'' for you, when all the truths you have ever heard suddenly seemed to be written in letters of fire for you, when suddenly the underlying meaning of things began to come through to you.

You may not remember when your spiritual

awakening began, or you may be able to remember the very hour in which the light began to shine in you and for you. But whether or not you remember, no one needs to tell you that the remembrance of the time is not the vital thing; it is the living and growing that you have done since then that you praise and give thanks for now.

Just as no one but you can celebrate your birthday—it is your own special day—certainly no one but you can celebrate your spiritual birth. The day of your physical birth is a matter of record. Your family, your friends help you celebrate; they think of you with love and affection on your special day. But no other person in the world knows your spiritual birthday. It is between you and God; it is a knowledge of the soul, a secret of the spirit. It is *the mystery hidden for ages and generations . . . which is Christ in you, the hope of glory.* (Col. 1:26-27)

Our birthday but hints at the truth about us; it merely tells that we were born into the world on a certain day, in a certain year. It does not tell when we began to live; it does not reveal our spiritual progress. Our birthday is a date on the calendar, but our birth into Truth is a continual never-ceasing process.

When you wish a friend or a dear one a happy birthday, do not stop in your thoughts with just good wishes. Do not send only your love and blessings, but add to these wishes your silent recognition of the truth about him, your silent realization that as dear as he may be to you, as well as you may know him, still there is a self of him that has passed through wildernesses you know nothing of; there is a self of him that has grown in ways you cannot imagine; there is a self of him that stands glorious and free, that is ageless, deathless, eternal.

When you say "Happy birthday" to someone, give thanks in your heart for God's Spirit in him. Give thanks in your heart for the indwelling Christ in him and in all of us. Give thanks for the freeing Truth, which is at work in every mind and heart in ways known only to the individual and his own indwelling Lord.

When it is your birthday, open your heart and mind and life to the goodwill of the universe. And especially open your heart and mind and life to the love of your Father-God. He who created you and sent you forth has never left you. He loves you with an everlasting love. He says to the self of you that understands: "I am always with you. You are my beloved child, in whom I am well pleased."

And on your birthday, no matter if you celebrate in an outer way or not, no matter if anyone else knows it is your birthday, make it an inner celebration of your spiritual awakening. Think of the overcomings you have made, of the growth you have made, of the times and ways in which God has made Himself known to you. Think of your birthday as a turning point in your life; think of it as a day in which you realize anew that you are beloved, needed, important, a day in which you realize anew that you live in eternal life.

God bless you on your birthday!

Retirement—a Turning Point

Anyone facing retirement from a job, either by choice or because of company policy, is certainly at a turning point.

A person may be looking forward eagerly to retirement. Still, as the time approaches, he may be filled with many conflicting thoughts and emotions.

The one who does not want to retire, who is resistant to the whole idea of it, has, of course, much greater inner conflict, and he may find himself re-acting with irritation, even anger, to persons and situations because of his feelings of fear and insecurity.

Even the person who looks forward to retirement may not like the connotation of the word. No one wants to think of himself as old or useless or un-needed.

I have always liked what May Rowland had to say about the word *retirement*. She was looking for-ward to retiring from her many years as director of Silent Unity, but did not like the word *retirement*. She said that as she thought about it, it came to her that when you re-tire a car, you put on new tires so that you can get going. This gave her a positive thought about retirement.

Getting rid of the feeling that we are old is an important part of making retirement a turning point in the right direction.

If we allow ourselves to think in terms of age, it would almost seem that we are never at the ''right'' age. When we are children, we can hardly wait to grow up. Then there may be a time in our lives when we are considered too young for some respon-sibility, or not mature enough. Before we realize what has happened, we have crossed an invisible line, and then we are considered too old.

You see what can happen if we fall in line with this idea of age! The great people of the world have always ignored chronological age. Jesus was too young, by the world's standards, to have made an impact on peoples' lives and thought that was to change the course of history. Michaelangelo was "too old," in his eighties, to be painting the Sistine Chapel ceiling! Grandma Moses was in her seventies—certainly "too old" to teach herself to paint.

Age is a matter of consciousness. An idea that has helped me is this: "I am neither old nor young. I am Spirit." We can learn to think of ourselves as Spirit, as on a continuing journey in life. We may have lived many years, but that does not make us old. We may have much behind us, but we also have much before us.

One thing that keeps us young in spirit is the ability to change. We may have become so identified with a business or a job that we cannot imagine ourselves spending our days in any other way. Perhaps this will be one of the happy things we will discover about retirement: while it may be the end of a particular job, it is the beginning of a new and interesting phase of life.

Most of us have said or thought that if only we had the time, we would like to pursue some field of study or develop some latent talent. Perhaps we have thought that if only we had the time, we would follow through on some project that we started but never completed. Retirement can give us time to learn and grow in new and fascinating ways.

Some persons may feel that retirement is the end of the world, the end of their life. Of course, it isn't, any more than their first job was the beginning of their world or the beginning of their life!

Retirement is just one of the many experiences in life. An important experience, it is true; a fearful experience to some, it is true. But retirement, while it may affect the pattern of your life, cannot and does not affect your spiritual identity.

Let me repeat: *Retirement cannot and does not affect your spiritual identity.*

With retirement you may have a sense of displacement. You may feel that the identity you have built up through your work, through your progress in your field, through the years of success (and yes, some failure), is now threatened. In spite of testimonial dinners and gold watches and praise from your coworkers, you may feel rejected. You may feel unwanted, you may feel that you have been put on the shelf.

If you have such feelings, they are temporary; they are passing. What has been put on the shelf, as far as you are concerned, is just one phase of your existence—your job.

But you, the child of God, are not on the shelf. Your spiritual identity is intact. You are needed, you are important. You are ready for a change, that is all. This is the most important thing you can know.

You are a unique, important creation of God. You are needed by Him. Retirement from one job does not absolve you of participation in life. It does not take away anything from your true purpose and place in life.

When the day you retire actually arrives, you are going to discover that, like many things you have dreaded and hoped would never happen, retirement is not as bad as you led yourself to expect. It may take you a little time to get used to the idea of retirement, but do not become discouraged. You have a resilient, resourceful spirit in you that enables you to meet change and then, without too much backward looking, go forward to meet the good that awaits you.

You may wonder what you will do with the new way of life that retirement will open to you. Certainly as you go forward with a feeling of confidence, as you hold to the realization that you are more than a job, more than a paycheck, that you are a child of God, the days and the years ahead will be happy and profitable ones.

God is and always has been the source of your supply. His supply has many channels through which it manifests itself. God's supply is not limited.

God never retires, and God is in you. God never fears, and God is in you. God never fails, and God is in you.

So, one job is behind you! All of life is ahead of you and there is much for you to do, much for you to enjoy in the Father's kingdom.

There is happiness for you.

There is something new for you in every day, for every day is God's day. Every day you have but to look for it, and you will see so much of good that you will marvel at the fears of yesterday. You will see how false they proved to be, and how true it is that God's good never comes to an end!

Alone, Perhaps. Lonely—Never!

If there is one feeling that most people have at one time or another, it is the feeling of loneliness. With most of us it is only an occasional or fleeting feeling. With some it is a devastating feeling, a feeling that can become almost overpowering.

Why this loneliness? Probably it is because each of us is essentially alone, however surrounded by other people we may be. No matter how close we may feel to another person, there is a part of us that is separate and apart, there is a part of us that no one else shares.

We are lonely until we realize (though we may have thought we knew it!) that we are never alone, that God is within us, that though we shut our door at night and put out the light, still we are never alone. God is with us! His presence is with us; His light shines within us. When we realize that we are never alone, that day or night, in the midst of a crowd or in solitude, God is with us, we no longer feel lost or alone. And paradoxically, we seem to draw people and happy experiences to ourselves.

If you feel lonely, be thankful! Not because you

are lonely, but because the fact that you are lonely indicates a capacity in you for caring and sharing!

If you feel lonely, if you long for companionship, then you are not one who has withdrawn into your shell. You are basically loving and outgoing. You do not want to shut people out of your life. In your cry of loneliness, you are reaching out, and in your reaching out, you are opening the way, putting out the welcome sign for a happy response.

There are many, many lonely people in the world, and they are lonely for a variety of reasons. A person may be surrounded by people and still be lonely if the one person to whom he felt closest is no longer with him. He is lonely, not because of a lack of friends, but because of the loss of one person who had become almost a part of him. Can such loneliness be overcome? It can be and has been by many people.

As difficult as it is for such people to accept the fact that life must go on, that they must put themselves into life, they discover that they are able to do this. They find that the love they have cherished is not really lost, that all they have gained through sharing the love of another person helps them to understand and reach out to others now.

Loneliness is a feeling of not relating to others, of

not really being a part of their lives. There is the mother, for instance, who lives with her grown children. Even in the midst of a busy family household, she may feel very alone, because she feels unneeded and unwanted. It is not easy to be in this position. However, the loneliness can be alleviated if such a person will begin to think of herself as a spiritual being, rather than just as a mother and a grandmother, if she will begin to affirm that she is needed and important to God and His scheme of things. How she relates to God, how she relates to herself has more to do with her feeling of loneliness than the circumstances in which she finds herself. Many times the great need is to make friends *with* ourselves if we are lonely.

There is a difference between being alone and being lonely. There are some persons whom we never think of as lonely. Though they live alone they seem a part of life, they are vital and alive, they are interested in what is going on around them.

Silent Unity has helped many persons to overcome loneliness, first of all by teaching them that they are never alone, that God is with them. And then by inviting these persons to join Silent Unity in praying for others. Prayer is a great unifier.

When we pray with others, we feel close to them, though miles separate us, and even if we never see them.

The light in the Silent Unity window has become a lovely symbol of togetherness. People have written to say that when they wake in the night they think of the lighted window. They remember that someone is praying, and they do not feel alone.

James Dillet Freeman says that Silent Unity is the friend who is always there. This is a great help to those who feel lonely—to know that someone cares, that someone is always there, that they have friends who are with them in Spirit, who are praying with them, who believe in them.

If you are lonely, the temptation may be to feel sorry for yourself, to begin to doubt your worth, to condemn or blame yourself. If you find yourself thinking along such lines, stop right there and remind yourself of who and what you are. You are God's beloved child; you have His Spirit in you. Your life is an expression of His life; your heart is filled with His love. Say to yourself: *God loves me. God has faith in me. God needs me. God is with me now. I am never alone.*

Just the mere saying of these words will not take away all the loneliness, will not instantly change conditions in your life, but just saying such words will help tremendously. For such words will help to change the trend of your thinking and feeling. They will take you back to the realization of yourself as a spiritual being, as a needed and important part of God's perfect plan.

Some persons find it helpful to say upon opening their eyes in the morning: _Something good is going to happen to me today._ One friend had a favorite little verse that she said upon awaking:

"Every morning I will say,

Something happy is on the way."

These are not magical ideas, but they are thought-brighteners. They are good starters for a day. They are welcoming words, for they open the mind and heart and life to a feeling of expectancy, to a feeling of joy in living, to a revived sense of wonder.

Alone, perhaps. Lonely, never! Let this be your keynote. Always God is with you; always you are one in Spirit, not only with God but with all humanity. We may walk apart; we do not walk alone.

III

A Turning Point:
When We Behold the Christ in Others

===

What About Others?

What about others? How are we to help them? The age-old question is, "Am I my brother's keeper?"

When someone close to us—perhaps a relative or a friend—is having financial difficulties and turns to us for help, what are we to do? Shall we give him the money he asks for? In some cases yes, in other cases no.

We do not help another if we relieve him of his own responsibilities, if we make it easy for him to use money foolishly or unwisely by being there with a handout when he asks for it. There are those who have never learned to use good judgment in handling their money or affairs. Someone has always been found to bail them out at the last minute. If we have tried to help such a person by giving him money, we have found how little help we were after all.

There are times, of course, when our help is needed, when what we are able to do for someone makes the difference in whether or not he is able to go on and find his way through some unexpected difficulty.

How are we to know when we are helping or not helping? How are we to feel right within ourselves if we give help or withhold it?

Whether we help another person materially is a question we must decide for ourselves, and we need to pray to be guided not only by a spirit of love and compassion but by a spirit of wisdom and understanding.

What we are to remember is that material help is never enough, that it is never the answer, except temporarily, to another person's needs. We do have a responsibility when another person comes to us for help. This responsibility is to pray for that one and to behold in that person the Spirit of God, the loving provider, the omnipresent answer to all his needs.

Peter said to the lame man who asked alms of him: *"I have no silver and gold, but I give you*

*what I have; in the name of Jesus Christ of Naza-
reth, walk.''* (Acts 3:6) What he had to give were
words of life, words of power, a prayer spoken in
the name of Jesus Christ that set the man free and
enabled him to stand on his feet again.

The greatest help we can give another is to have
faith in him, to pray for him, to realize that he has
the Spirit of God within him that is powerful to
change and transform him and his life.

No one wants to feel dependent on others. No
one really wants to be in a position of asking someone else to take over his responsibilities. Many
times the person who attempts to take over another
person's life, to relieve him of his need to meet life
for himself, finds that the one he has helped does
not appreciate what he has done, and may, in fact,
resent him for it.

Many letters come to Silent Unity from those
who are concerned about a relative or a dear one
who seems to be in great need. Perhaps these people who are writing say they have exhausted their
own resources trying to help the other person. It
turns out that they have not, despite their help,
solved the other person's problems, and they want
to know what they can do. They want Silent Unity
to pray for them and to pray for the one whose

life is in such a muddled state.

Then we may hear later from someone who has written us in such a situation. He may say, as one man did, "I can only say that it is a miracle!" This man's brother had for years been going downhill in every way. He had a drinking problem, was without work, and had broken family relations. The man had written to Silent Unity for prayers for his brother, and had sent the brother a subscription to *DAILY WORD*. He had not heard from his brother for several years, but happened to pass through the town where the brother lived. He could hardly believe the change that had taken place in him. He had joined Alcoholics Anonymous, had found work, and the whole picture of his life had changed. The friend who wrote us about it said that while his brother did not credit prayer with all of it, he told him that the turning point in his life came with the first copy of *DAILY WORD*.

If you are troubled about some dear one, if you have tried to help in outer ways and it has seemed in vain, perhaps your need now is to release the feeling that it is all up to you. It takes a great deal of faith to believe, really believe, that the one who seems to have gotten himself and his life into a state of chaos has the power within him to make a new start, to change the direction of his life. Looking at outer appearances, it may not seem possible, but if we can <u>look to the spiritual self and keep our faith in the power of God in the one about whom we are concerned</u>, we can help the person far beyond anything we have yet been able to do.

When we are concerned about another, when we long to help, our prayers are needed by that person, but first of all, <u>*we* need our prayers</u>. We need to lift up our vision, we need to pray for understanding and guidance. We need to let go of any feeling that he is a poor, incapable creature, let go of the belief that this dear one is our responsibility alone. We may be part of the answer, but he *(I)* <u>is God's child and God's responsibility.</u> We need to trust God to work in and through him to change and transform and make all things right in his *my* life.

Are we our brothers' keeper? Yes, if by that we mean that we are to love others. We are to have faith in them; we are to support them spiritually; we are to see them as God sees them; we are to behold the Christ in them. This is the way we truly help others; this is the help they truly want from us.

The Stranger in Our Midst

The accounts of Jesus' reappearance after the Resurrection ring true, because the tendency of one imagining such an event would be along spectacular lines.

Here is the Savior who has been cruelly treated and condemned to death ignominiously. Now He reappears, proof that He is indeed the Son of God as He claimed, and king of the world.

Would not the imagination dramatize this appearance? If angels appeared in shining white, surely He would be a shining, triumphant figure. He would so astonish and astound that people would be blinded by His appearance and fall down at His feet and worship Him.

But the account as it is told is not like this at all. It has a ring of authenticity. Mary mistook Jesus for the gardener, not a blazing figure of light and glory. She saw a simple figure of a man, standing there as if he belonged among the growing things.

The two disciples on their way to Emmaus met up with a traveler and walked and talked with him for miles, telling him about the sad events in Jerusalem in the previous days. Was Jesus trying to disguise Himself? I think not. We can believe more readily in His resurrection when we see Him as a man we would walk and talk with, listen to and love.

Since Jesus' resurrection there have been accounts of His reappearance time and again as the stranger who seemed to appear out of nowhere, who left such an impact on the lives He touched that people wondered after He had disappeared: "Who was this man? Who was this stranger in our midst?"

We have all read such accounts; we have read many stories based on this theme of the Stranger, the Christ, in our midst. But if we wait for some mysterious stranger to appear out of nowhere, we may fail to recognize the Christ, as surely as did the woman at the tomb or the two on the road to Emmaus.

The gardener, the stranger on the road—do they not symbolize everyone? The Christ we do not recognize may be found in the one we pass by or even turn away from.

If we have longed to see the Christ, perhaps we have not looked for Him where He is to be found. When Jesus' disciples wanted to see the Father, He said: *". . . He who has seen me has seen the*

Father . . . .'' (John 14:9) He also said: *"I and the Father are one."* (John 10:30) He made it clear that the God presence was not only in Him but in us. *"I in them and thou in me, that they may become perfectly one . . . ."* (John 17:23)

Jesus was telling us where to look for the Christ when He said: *" '. . . I was hungry and you gave me food, I was thirsty and you gave me drink, I was a stranger and you welcomed me, I was naked and you clothed me, I was sick and you visited me, I was in prison and you came to me.' . . . 'Truly, I say to you, as you did it to one of the least of these my brethren, you did it to me.' "* (Matt. 25:35-40)

One of the most meaningful phrases in the Unity teachings is, "I behold the Christ in you." Frank B. Whitney used this phrase in his poem "I Behold the Christ in You." This phrase has become a living prayer. It has helped people to open their eyes to see the Christ in others. It has been a way of looking at persons that has been a healing benediction.

We may look at a person and see him as sick or weak, we may see him as lacking in judgment or wisdom, we may see him as selfish or cruel. This is judging by appearances. When we try, even in a small way, to behold the Christ in another, what a difference it makes! Not necessarily in him, but in us!

If we have found it difficult to release hurt or resentment because of what someone has said or done, when we lift our thoughts, lift our vision, and pray this prayer, "I behold the Christ in you," healing comes. We are able to release bitter feelings and unloving thoughts. We see something in that one we did not see before. We appreciate something in him we did not appreciate before. Now we behold the Christ in him, and beholding the Christ we are able to forgive and bless him.

Many people have told us of the almost miraculous change that took place in some relationship, in some situation when they held to this idea, "I behold the Christ in you." One woman said that a man had owed her husband money for a long time and ignored the matter completely. Her husband had shrugged it off, but the woman had become so bitter in her thoughts toward the man and so resentful that they had to do without things they needed that it was making her physically ill. She decided that she would take some time every day to pray for the man and to use these words, "I behold the Christ in you." Needless to say, this prayer helped her to release feelings of resentment and injustice, which was a great blessing in itself. And it was not long until the man came to her husband, saying that he wanted to pay the long-standing debt.

If we wish there were better people in the world, let us remember something essential, which is that wherever we look, we are beholding the Christ. We are looking into the face of Christ as we look into the face of humanity.

When we see Christ in all and through all, our eyes will be opened. We will know that we have seen the Christ.

"I behold the Christ in you." These words can change our outlook on life; these words can change our world. Christ is in us and in all men, our "hope of glory."

Christ is no longer the stranger in our midst; we recognize Him everywhere. We find Him in ourselves; we behold Him in others.

In the Faces of Children

When we look at children, what do we see? Do we see our child, grandchild, niece, or nephew?

Do we see a nose like the father's, a smile like the mother's?

Yes, this is a way of looking at children, but if this is the only way we look at them, then we do not really see them. We are seeing them as projections of ourselves and our families, not as they really are.

Every child is a unique creation, drawn to this particular place in life, at this particular time. He looks like his family, perhaps, but he is a brand-new creation.

He does not fit into a mold; rather he has his own pattern to unfold. He has his own destiny to fulfill, his own reason for being, his own place in God's perfect scheme of things.

How can we help children express their inherent greatness? How can we help them to enter into life without fear? How can we help them to keep their childlike wonder, their total trust, their unquestioning faith, their capacity for love?

There are many things we can teach our children, and there are many things we teach them without being aware of it. We do not need to teach a child to love; children come into the world with an instinct for love. They respond to the warmth of a loving atmosphere, to loving words, naturally and happily. Children bring love into the world—and they are happy children when they find themselves in a climate of love.

This is what we can give our children that is unique with us. No matter how many books we read on child care, no matter how many courses we take in child psychology, the magic ingredient in caring for a child, in helping a child, is love.

Just as every child has an inherent capacity for love, so do we. We were once the little child, looking at the world with love and trust. The same love and trust are in us now. The children in our lives remind us of this and we are more loving because of what they draw forth from us.

Children need approval and encouragement. We do not need to be told this. We know it, because we have this same need. We are simply further along the road. We need approval and encouragement for different things.

As a parent or teacher or an adult to whom the child looks, our approval and encouragement are important and necessary. We can help the child to learn many things he needs to know in order to live successfully and happily, and we can do this without making him dependent upon us. What we want for him is that he learn to think for himself, that he find his own way, that he learn to act from his own inner convictions. When he feels that we are one with him, that we love him, that we approve of him, he will be free to expand his abilities and use his latent intelligence.

Children are born believers. We can help them keep a feeling of faith alive in their hearts by keeping our own faith alive.

When we look at the child and see him as a child of God, as a child of light, we bless him and help him in ways that are beyond anything we could say or do.

Faith is inherent in us, even as love is inherent. We know from our own experience how a few people along the way have represented such great faith to us that our own faith was strengthened because of them.

The more we trust in the goodness of God, in the goodness of life, in the Spirit of God at work in human minds and hearts and lives, the more we help our children to develop and maintain a faith of their own.

Parents, above all things, want their children to be happy. They try to give the children happiness; sometimes they try to buy happiness for their children. They think that things can bring smiles to little faces, which they do. But every parent knows in his heart that he really makes his child happy when he gives of himself to the child, when he gives of his time and interest and enthusiasm.

The child with a few playthings may be infinitely happier than the child with many. Happiness is a state of mind, as we all well know. We know that we feel the happiest when we feel needed and loved, when we forget self and enter wholeheartedly into life.

We cannot give our children happiness. We cannot buy happiness for our children. We can add to our child's happiness; we can increase our child's happiness by doing anything we can to help him be what he is meant to be—a giving, loving, growing child of God.

All parents dream great dreams for their children. We look at the baby in the crib, staring at us so solemnly, and we are awed. Here is a new life, here is a new person.

What will this child's life be like? What direction will it take? What kind of world will the child grow up in? We may wish that this child of ours had some sort of fairy godmother who could wave a magic wand and insure only good things in his or her life forever and ever.

This child of ours has something better than a fairy godmother—every child has. This child, every child, has the very <u>Spirit of God within.</u> This Spirit is the great and wonderful Spirit that is with him in the cradle, that brought him forth into life. This Spirit in him has created him perfect.

The child lives in the holy temple of God; God's life fills every cell; God's light shines in his mind; God's power moves in and through him.

The potential for greatness that is in our child surpasses anything we can envision for him. The presence of God that is always with him insures good things for him now and through all the days of his life.

When we look into the faces of children and think of them as children of God, we see them in an entirely different way. We feel a sense of wonder when we think of all they brought with them into life, when we think of all that lies before them. And we can be glad that they are a part of our lives, that we are a part of their lives. In them and in us, the Christ looks forth and smiles upon the world.

A Day We All Are Children

Mother's Day is a day we take for granted. At least I did. I had not thought much about it, except to think of it as a nice occasion for remembering one's mother. When I was asked to give a talk on Mother's Day, I began thinking about it and what it had to say to me, or to anyone, for that matter.

How did Mother's Day begin? I asked one young mother and she said, "I believe a young man must have started it." It so happens that she has a seven-year-old boy, and I think she was hoping that this is the way he would feel.

I asked another person, "How do you think Mother's Day began?" He said, "Probably the greeting card companies started it!"

The fact is that Mother's Day began as an idea in the mind of one woman, Miss Ann Jarvis, of Philadelphia. She was of middle age when she lost her mother on May 9, 1906. On the same day a year later, she met with a friend to commemorate her mother. She confided in her friend that she had the idea of a national Mother's Day, a day when everyone would remember his or her mother in some way and honor her. She was thinking especially of adult children. This idea became a consuming one with her. She wrote thousands of letters and contacted all sorts of people who might be influential in getting her idea across. By the following year, 1908, Philadelphia celebrated Mother's Day on the second Sunday in May.

In 1913 the House of Representatives and the Senate of the United States passed a resolution, setting aside the second Sunday in May as Mother's Day, a day to honor all mothers, especially one's own. Ann Jarvis continued to be a driving force behind this idea of Mother's Day until it spread to other countries as well.

Unfortunately, some people celebrate Mother's Day because they feel remorseful and regretful. Perhaps they have not let their mothers know how much they appreciate and love them. They may feel guilt over things said or not said. They may feel that in some way they have neglected their mothers. These are not uncommon feelings and are often a source of great grief. In most cases such feelings are unwarranted, and in many instances, the one who feels that he has not done enough may be the one who has been utterly devoted.

Because no human relationship measures up to the perfect ideal of love, we feel that we have failed. When we think about ourselves and our lives, we know that no person in the world can truly satisfy all our needs and desires, all our inner longings; that only as we live close to God and let His Spirit find expression through us do we find happiness, peace, and satisfaction. We would not want someone else to feel remorseful because we are not completely at peace, completely happy, completely successful, would we? We know that our answer does not lie outside ourselves, does not rest with other persons, but with God, with ourselves.

It helps us to overcome grief when we realize this and are able to release and bless those who pass from one phase of soul experience to another. We see them as children of God, and we keep faith in them as children of God.

However, I think we learn something else from the story of Ann Jarvis, for after Mother's Day had been adopted and the idea had spread even to other countries, she became bitter because she did not think it was being observed the way she had envisioned. She felt that it had become commercialized, and even went into litigation, trying to rescind the whole idea.

In a sense, this was her child, this idea of Mother's Day. She had given birth to it, nurtured it, fostered it, and had seen it come of age. But on its own, the idea became something she had not anticipated.

This is something we learn as mothers—whether of children, of projects, of ideas. We cannot hold them to ourselves or limit them or bind them, but must let them mature and stand on their own.

Dorothy Canfield Fisher said: *A mother is not a person to lean on but a person to make leaning unnecessary.*

All mothers hope to help their children learn to be on their own, to find and express their own potential. But it is not always easy to allow children freedom to live their own lives. When children are small they need parental guidance, of course, but sometimes we cannot let go of our grownup children.

We may become miserable and unhappy because our grownup children are not doing the things we think they should or living their lives the way we think they should. We may find that if we offer our advice, it is not welcome. It may not be easy to accept, but we have to be willing to allow our children freedom to stand on their own, freedom to live their own lives. We have to be willing to trust the Spirit of God in them to direct and inspire them. When we do this, our relationship with our children changes. Instead of being a demanding, possessive one, it becomes a happy, free one, in which we and our children are blessed. We come to understand and appreciate one another as individuals, growing and unfolding according to our own inner light.

Mother's Day, like most holidays, is a day for remembering. Our thoughts go back to childhood days. The mother-child relationship stays with us always. To our mothers, even if we are grown and married, with children and perhaps grandchildren, we are always children. Once Rose Kennedy appeared on a television special and talked about John F. Kennedy—not the president but the little boy, who was sometimes obstreperous, who did not always do the things he was supposed to do. Only Rose Kennedy would have had this little boy in mind when she talked about John F. Kennedy!

Mother's Day is a day we all are children, but it is a day also to think of ourselves as children in a broader sense—children of God. We are children of God first and foremost—including our mothers—and members of the great family of God. I think Jesus was talking about this when He said: *"Who is my mother, and who are my brothers? . . . Here are my mother and my brothers! For whoever does the will of my Father in heaven is my brother, and sister, and mother."* (Matt. 12:48-50) In other words, the family relationship is broader than we think it is. In a sense, we are one with all people and all people are related to us.

Mother's Day is not just for mothers. It is a day for all of us—men, women, and children. It is a day to think about some of these things, as well as to remember our mothers.

The Fifth Commandment is: *"Honor your father and your mother . . . ."* (Exod. 20:12) To honor means to respect, to regard with high esteem, to reverence, to stand in awe of. The word *honor* is a rather forbidding one. We can honor someone we do not even know. We can honor someone we do not love. We can honor someone we do not understand.

Jesus said: *"A new commandment I give to you, that you love one another . . . ."* (John 13:34) Perhaps this is the new commandment as to mothers: that we are to honor them, of course, but that we are to go beyond that—we are to love them.

This can be a day to express love, to your mother

and to others. If your mother is no longer here so you can express that love, you can honor her on this day by expressing love to someone, by letting someone know that he or she is loved and appreciated, that you think he or she is a special, beautiful person.

Perhaps this is the real message of Mother's Day, that we are to express the love we feel. We will not have regrets; we will not say, "I wish I had told this person how I felt about him" or, "If only I had told her how much I loved her," if we resolve to do it now.

"Who is my mother?" There are mothers by reason of birth, there are adoptive mothers, there are foster mothers, there are ones who have acted as mother substitutes.

We have many mothers in another sense. Those who have nurtured our hopes and dreams, those who have taught us, encouraged us, inspired us— these are our mothers, too.

Some of the world's greatest mothers, in the universal sense of the word, have never borne children of their own, but have devoted their lives to others. *Her children rise up and call her blessed.* (Prov. 31:28) There are those who have "children" all over the world who love and appreciate them because of their contribution to life.

When we think about the people who have had an influence on our lives, we think about teachers, about friends, about relatives. I suppose all of us have had a teacher we remember. For me, a third-grade teacher comes to mind. Her name was Martha Persis Smith. The thing I remember about her is that every morning the class stood up and said in unison, ''Wearing the white flower of a blameless life.'' I am sure that none of us had any idea what it was all about or what we were saying, but somehow it must have given the little children in that class a larger vision of themselves and life. I didn't know till many years later that this quotation was from Tennyson.

Hannah More Kohaus wrote ''The Prayer of Faith,'' and I grew up with this prayer. I do not know anything about Hannah More Kohaus, but I think she must have been one of my mothers. Children are still learning it and living with it, so whether or not she had any children of her own, she has many children everywhere.

H. Emilie Cady never had children, but in her way she was a mother to perhaps millions, for through her book *Lessons in Truth* she changed my life and the lives of countless others. She showed us something about ourselves we did not know by showing us the spiritual side of our nature.

All of us can think of people who have been part of our mothering, who have helped and encouraged us along the way. Mother's Day is a day to think of them with appreciation, to give thanks for them.

To me, Silent Unity is the mothering side of the Unity work. Like a mother, Silent Unity prayer help is there when you need it. The light is always shining in the window. People write to Silent Unity or call on it as they would a mother. They pour out their souls, knowing that prayer help will be given and that what they have written or called about will be held in confidence and not passed along or discussed with anyone. I think this is a wonderful, mothering idea.

Silent Unity receives many letters and telephone calls from children. Not long ago a little boy called Silent Unity. A man who was on duty answered. The little boy didn't say anything for a minute, and the man said again: "Silent Unity. May we help you?" Again silence, and then the little boy said, "Could I please speak to *Mrs.* Silent Unity?" He may have thought it would be easier to talk to someone more like a mother!

If some mothers become possessive in their love for their children and are unwilling to allow them freedom to grow and unfold according to the divine plan within them, so do some children reverse the role and become very possessive of their mothers. They want their mothers to be in their image and to act according to their idea of what a mother should be.

There was once a play on television called "The Queen of the Stardust Ballroom." It was about a middle-aged woman who had lost her husband. She felt very lonely. The children wanted her to live with them but she did not want to. She was rather plain looking—colorless hair, drab clothes—with an air of dejection. Then a friend induced her to go with her to the Stardust Ballroom, which opened a whole new world to her. She had her hair tinted, learned how to wear makeup, and bought some new clothes. Her daughter came to visit her and was shocked. She said: "Mother, you look awful! What will I tell your grandchildren?" The mother calmly replied, "Tell them that I feel like a movie star!"

I think there is a point here. Each of us has to allow his or her mother to live her life, to be herself, to go the way that Spirit leads her and not try to put her into a mold that fits our particular way of thinking.

Perhaps "honor your mother" means honoring her right to be a person, honoring the wonderful Spirit of God in her, honoring her right to live her own life. This is what you want from her; this is what she wants from you.

And what mothers want above all, what all of us want above all, is to be loved, to feel that someone understands us, that someone believes in us.

Our prayer on Mother's Day might be: "Loving Father-Mother God, we thank You that we are Your children, one with one another in love, growing together in love, finding our way to happiness and understanding in a oneness of heart, mind, and spirit."

IV

A Turning Point:
When We Let God Work Through Us

Does It Just Happen?

Divine order. Does it just happen? Do we have something to do with it?

We know that we have something to do with order in our home, in our affairs. A house does not clean itself. Closets do not put themselves in order. Yard work does not get done by itself. Decisions are not made by themselves. A cluttered desk does not clear itself. Someone's attention and efforts are involved in the establishment of such order.

What about divine order, then? Is it a different kind of order?

I think not. If we accept the premise that God works through us, then we see that divine order is a result of letting God work through us, a result of getting ourselves in tune with His ever-present power within us.

These two words *divine order* have become key words with many people. I know that they are an almost automatic response with me in all kinds of situations.

Have you ever said to yourself "divine order" as you drove your car into a crowded shopping area, and just then, someone pulled out of the perfect parking spot? I have friends whom I always appreciate having with me when I drive, for I feel their affirmation of divine order, even if they do not say the words aloud, and the driving is always smooth and safe, and parking a pleasure.

There is nothing magic about these two words *divine order,* but at times the effect is such, like the time my teenage daughter and I were planning to drive somewhere. Our garage has automatic overhead doors. Only this time when I pressed the button, nothing happened. My daughter said, "Now, what are we going to do?" I said, "Divine order." With the skepticism of youth, and especially of the wisdom of one's own parent, she said, "You know, Mother, you are not magic." With that I pressed the button again, and the door went up! Of course, it was not magic, but I firmly believe that somehow my affirmation of divine order helped release whatever was obstructing the operation of that door.

One time when we were living in Philadelphia, I had an important appointment. As I tried to start the car, the motor would not turn over. It seemed dead. The woman who was cleaning our house that day came to the door and said, "Mrs. Smock, can I help you?" I said: "No, Eva, I'm declaring divine order." With that I turned the ignition and the car started. I was on my way! When I returned, Eva met me at the door and said, "What was the power word you spoke?" I said, "Divine order." She said, "Well, we need it again, the air conditioner isn't working!"

Eva took hold of the idea of divine order and told me a few months later how she and her husband were driving from New York one night. It was late and no filling stations were open. They began to have car trouble, and her husband said they would never make it home. She kept declaring divine order, and they made it home without having to stop.

When we affirm divine order, what are we affirming? I think that first of all we are affirming something about ourselves. We are affirming that we are in tune, that we are in divine order in our inner selves. We are affirming divine order in our thoughts and feelings, divine order in our attitudes, divine order in our ability to discern needed steps, divine order in our use of good judgment. We tune in, as it were, to the overall idea of divine order, which is another word for the power of God at work. In this oneness with God's power, we become channels through which this power flows. It may be in small matters, it may be in some very important and life-changing matter.

But like the desk drawer that remains cluttered unless we act to straighten it out, like the home that remains dusty and disorderly unless we do something to set it in order, like the office project that remains unfinished unless we follow through on whatever needs to be done to complete it, divine order does not just happen.

The establishment of divine order may not entail any outer effort on our part, but it always entails some spiritual effort. It entails our willingness to trust in the good outworking of things; it entails our willingness to release anxiety and tension and the feeling that we are personally responsible for the solution of some situation. It entails our belief in the omnipresence of God, our belief in the ultimate goodness of His plan for us and for all His creation. Behind these two words *divine order* are some large beliefs and ideas!

I think the reason *divine order* as an affirmation has caught hold, has captured the interest and imagination of so many people, is that it sums up in two words an affirmative outlook on life.

A friend told me, for instance, that she declared divine order when entering an operating room. To her divine order included not only her healing, but the guidance of doctors and nurses. Divine order included anyone or anything that had to do with her care and recovery. Divine order was a way of saying: "Father, I am in Your care. All is well."

I have used this idea of divine order when there has seemed to be some misunderstanding. It has helped me to stay poised, not to get upset, not to jump to conclusions. *Divine order.* Sometimes the affirming of this is another way of saying to myself: "Steady. God is in charge."

There may be times when we find ourselves in situations where we wish that we could do something to help set matters right, but we must stand by. Perhaps someone dear to us has some problem or need that, to us looking on, would seem to be simple to solve. But he has not asked our advice. Will our silently declaring divine order be of any help? It will. I know from experience. What it does first of all is to help us release our feeling that we should set this person's life straight, that we could show him the way if only he would listen. *Divine order.* This is what we want. "Not my will, but thine, be done." So we declare divine order, and in this affirmation of divine order we have the faith to know that the Spirit of God, the spirit of good, is at work in our dear one's life, that he has within him the power of God to guide and illumine him. God will reveal the right answer to him, in ways that he can understand, in ways that he can act upon, in ways that will be for his growth and good and happiness.

Divine order is a rightness, a right outworking of things, and this is what we are to affirm and hold to. Our affirmation of divine order may reveal to us what our part is in bringing about adjustment and right conditions in some situation. But even when there seems to be nothing we can do in an outer way to establish order in some confused and complex situation, our affirmation of divine order can be the positive word that acts as a catalyst to start changes in the right direction.

No, divine order does not just happen. We have our part in the establishment of it in our individual lives. However, the establishment of divine order does not depend on our efforts alone, but on our receptivity to the power of the indwelling Christ which is always at work in and through us and in and through all circumstances and conditions to make things right.

RSVP (Reply Requested)

You are invited! Oh, you may not receive an engraved invitation, there may be no RSVP, but you are invited—and a reply is requested!

Life invites you to participate. God invites you to partake of His good. Have you accepted or declined or merely ignored the invitation?

How does life invite you? How do you accept such an invitation? Life's invitations are hardly ever conventional; they do not "request the honor of your presence." They are more than likely thrust upon you—perhaps by some happening or circumstance that seems far from inviting. Life's invitation to participate may be thrust into your hand by the grubby hand of a child; it may be silently given you by the longing look in a lonely person's eyes. Life may invite you to step forward with courage when everything in you wants to turn and run.

Sometimes life's invitation to participate finds us among the cinders and ashes like Cinderella. We may feel neglected or forlorn and think that it is impossible for us to enjoy life because we are the "stepchild." But like Cinderella, most of us still have our hopes and dreams and our faith that life can be better, that there is a way, there is an answer. Like Cinderella, all can be transformed— rags to riches, mice to horses, pumpkins to coaches. The fairy godmother who waves her magic wand is someone we all know—she is that spirit of faith and trust in us that keeps us keeping on. And the magic wand is a very real concept, for we do have something that is even better than a magic wand—we have the magic of believing. We have the power of right thinking that can transform and bless us and transform and change any appearance, any condition. The power of God is the greatest power in the world. And when we turn to God, when we turn our thoughts from fear and doubt and self-pity to a sudden clear realization of ourselves as children of God, beloved by Him, strong in His Spirit and guided by his light, we set marvelous changes into effect.

We all know this. We have all had experiences when we were faced with something that seemed beyond us, but in that hour, we held to faith in God and we were filled with inner peace and strength. We saw our way clear to do what had to be done; we were able to meet what had to be met. No one needed to tell us at such a time that faith and prayer are mighty powers. We knew it, we experienced it!

Every fairy story has elements of truth in it, and the story of Cinderella is no exception. It is the dream of everyone to be suddenly, magically transformed, to step forth in splendor and beauty, to be recognized for what he has innately known himself to be. We are children of God, and now and again we have sudden flashes of inspiration that make us know it and show it.

You are invited! You are invited to accept God's bountiful, wondrous good. Why do you ever turn this invitation down? Why does anyone?

Thou preparest a table before me
in the presence of my enemies . . . .

(Psalms 23:5)

God's good, His life, His supply, His love, His power are spread before us, in the presence of our "enemies" fear, ignorance, self-condemnation, unforgiveness. God does not withdraw His invitation or withhold His good because of the enemies we have brought to the table with us. We often reject the very good for which we long by allowing ourselves to continue in negative attitudes, by letting fear take hold in us, by giving way to doubt, to feelings of unworthiness or inadequacy.

The invitation stands! Our good is set before us. All it takes is a change of thought, determination to look up instead of down, willingness to turn our eyes away from what seems to be and to accept our good. When we pray for light, God shows us the way and fills us with a new heart and a new spirit.

Sometimes we do not answer life's invitation because we are too busy with our own personal affairs and have allowed ourselves to fall into ruts of thinking and living. We feel that we cannot possibly turn aside from duties and chores to really listen to other people, or to enter the lives of others with interest and enthusiasm. The perfectionist housekeeper may shut people out of her home; the businessman may lose touch with his family and feel cut off from them; the teacher may be so bound to the text that he or she never hears what the pupils have to say.

When we let ourselves become bound by routine

and ritual we are like the ones in Jesus' parable about the householder who had been invited to a banquet. When word was sent to them, "Come, for all is now ready," they suddenly thought of all kinds of excuses for not attending. One had bought a field and had to see to it. Another had bought some oxen and had to attend to them. Another had married a wife, so of course he couldn't come!

We have all known people who are very much alone, yet out of fear or timidity or lack of confidence they turn down invitations that would bring them into closer companionship with others. They tell themselves that they prefer isolation and withdrawal to risking entry into an atmosphere that may be strange or intimidating.

But life is a persistent inviter. Even when we refuse again and again to let ourselves be drawn out of a shell, to let ourselves feel happy and joyous and loving, to let ourselves feel a part of humanity—often life seems to say to us, "Come, for all is now ready," and pushes us forward. And the one little step we take in faith seems reinforced—as indeed it is—by the powerful and loving, upholding presence of God. We find that we are not alone, that God's invitation to us to partake of life, to partake of His blessings, comes to us accompanied by the assurance, "I am with you; I will be with you; I will not fail you nor forsake you."

You are invited! A reply is requested. It need only be a silent, "Yes, Lord." It need only be a willingness of heart and mind to partake of God's good and to share His good, His joy with others.

> You Have—
>   Time Enough
>   Strength Enough
>   Energy Enough

Have you ever thought or said, "I have so much before me to do that I hardly know where to begin"? Most of us have times when it seems that the demands and activities of everyday life mount. We feel crowded and pressed for time; we go to bed at night feeling weary, not from what we have been able to do but because of all that we have had to leave undone.

We know instinctively that this is not in order, that this is not the way a child of God should think or feel. We know that somehow our affairs should be handled smoothly, easily, without stress or strain; but we do not seem to have the answer.

When we find ourselves weary with the thought of all that we have to do, when we find ourselves resisting and resenting the demands made on us, procrastinating, putting off doing the things we know need to be done, should be done, then we need to stop and make a new beginning, take a new direction; for when we find ourselves at such a place it is an indication that we are out of touch with Spirit, out of tune with the harmonizing power of God.

Before we attempt to change ourselves or change the way we approach life and its needs and demands, our first step should be to take time to relax, to return to God, our Source, our Creator, in silent prayer. Everyone needs the renewal, the refreshment, the rebuilding that prayer affords. We do not realize how much we need times of quietness, times of withdrawal, times of contemplation and communion with God, until we try to do without them. We think we are too busy to take time to pray, that we cannot stop and rest and withdraw for a few moments from the outer pressures.

But there is nothing that revives us and renews us as does prayer; there is nothing that makes us able to do all the things that are before us to do, easily, perfectly, on time, and in order that can compare with the revitalizing power of prayer. Praying is like recharging a battery; it is like plugging in a light bulb to an electric current. We are charged with new life from our Source, we are infilled and infused with spiritual power.

Another good result of silent prayer, when we find ourselves tense and anxious and pressed for time, is that in the clear, calm contemplation of Truth, where we see ourselves as spiritual beings, where we feel God's presence, where we are lifted to a new level of thought and consciousness, we are able to view ourselves and our lives objectively. Sometimes we are able to see that we have been busy and occupied with nonessentials.

We want to live a creative, worthwhile, productive life, but we do not want to clutter our lives with unnecessary things any more than we want to clutter our homes with unnecessary objects. As we open our minds and hearts and lives to light and guidance, we are shown what is right and essential for us to do; we are given the wisdom and the strength to say no to those things that we now see as time-consuming but not important or needful.

We shall find that we have time for the things we want to accomplish as we do all things in the thought that the power of Spirit is working in and through us. It is helpful to begin our day with an affirmation such as: *I work with Spirit, and I accomplish all things easily, perfectly, on time, and in order.*

Prayer will help us to overcome the habit of procrastination. All of us have had the experience of finding something very difficult to do, or if not difficult, a job that we resisted doing because it was not pleasant or appealing to us. But the longer we put off the doing of it, the harder it became.

With God's help we can do the things we need to do; and we shall find that in doing them promptly and to the best of our ability, we gain a great sense of peace and freedom. We find that we have time for the things we want to do as we establish order in our thinking and follow through by doing all things with a sense of order and rightness.

How to Make Decisions Easily

One of the most difficult things for many persons to do is to make a decison. This is because they do not trust their own judgment; they are afraid of making a decision because they do not want to make a mistake or do something for which they may be criticized.

How happy any one of us should be if we were always sure of the right thing to do, if we were without fear or hesitation in meeting the issues of life!

From a human standpoint we may not always be able to see what the right answer is to some particular question; we may be unsure of our way when we find ourselves in unfamiliar circumstances, faced with decisions that seem beyond our ability to make. But when we do not see our way, when we do not know what to do, we are not powerless. We are not without help. Within each of us is the all-knowing Mind of God, the Mind that is all-wise, all-seeing, the Mind that is infinite, the Mind that is our source of light and understanding.

Sometimes we think how wonderful it is that God has given us a mind with which to think, to reason, to know, to understand. How more wonderful it is to realize that He has given us His own Mind, the Mind of Spirit!

When we realize this, we lift the level of our thinking. We do not limit ourselves to the little we may know or have learned; rather we open our minds to the Mind of God, to the spiritual ideas that fill the universe, that flow to us from the fountainhead of light.

If you ever find yourself thinking that you do not know very much, that you have not had the advantage of education or travel or other means of increasing knowledge, remind yourself that you have access to the greatest source of wisdom in the universe, that you have within you the Mind of God. As you open your mind to the Mind of God, new and true ideas will begin to flow in to you; your understanding will be quickened, your ability to learn and to retain knowledge will be increased.

In making decisions, even the simple, everyday decisions that all of us are called on to make, you will find it easy if you breathe a prayer of thanks to God for His all-knowing Mind that is within you.

You do not need to beg God to show you the way or to tell you what to do; you need only open your mind to His Mind and say in faith: *Let there be light.* The light is there within you, the wisdom is there within you, the divine knowledge is there within you.

Your need is to unify your mind with the Mind of God, to know that this Mind is making plain and clear your way.

There is within everyone a divine source of wisdom, a shining light of Truth.

When others ask us to tell them what to do, when they want us to help them decide what to do in some matter, we need to remember that they have the Mind of God within them. Rather than attempting to tell them what to do or what steps they should take, let us know that there is a Spirit in them that knows far better than anyone else (even better than they themselves) what is right for them, that knows what is for their highest good, and that is continually shining through them to make their way known to them.

All of us have had the experience of not knowing what to do, of not knowing which path to take, of wanting someone or something to give us a sign or show us the way. But in those times when we prayed in faith, when we surrendered our personal will to the higher will of God and prayed, "God, show me the way," the darkness lifted, and suddenly we knew our answer.

Always the Mind of God is in us, and always this Mind will guide and direct us in the way of our highest good.

What You and God Can Do

There is an old story about a man who took over a ramshackle farmhouse and a run-down farm. He set to work to put the house in shape; he worked on the land, weeding and seeding, tilling and cultivating it. It was not long before results began to show. One day a minister drove by and stopped to admire the place. He said, "It's wonderful what you and God have done here." The man replied, "Yes, but you should have seen it when God had it alone!"

God has given us great potential for good, and He has given us the power, the spirit, and the will to bring forth this good in tangible ways in our lives. The story of the farmer illustrates this point. The potential to make something of the farm was within him; the potential to produce was within the farm; the potential, put to work, made something worthwhile out of something that seemed valueless.

When we look at whatever is before us that needs to be changed or improved, we should never feel helpless or discouraged. As we set to work in any way that presents itself to us to improve conditions, we shall see results, results that surpass our efforts, for we find that when we make a constructive effort, the forces of good are on our side. The circumstances and conditions that seemed immovable or impossible change before our eyes.

All of us admire and respect the person who does what is before him to do with a willingness of spirit, who does it to the best of his ability, who does it without grumbling or complaint. We do not feel sorry for him; he does not feel sorry for himself.

Even more do we like ourselves when we work in this attitude and spirit. This is the cure for frustration, for boredom, for self-pity. The housewife who tackles the breakfast dishes, makes the beds, and does the other sometimes monotonous morning tasks, likes herself better than the one who sits and stares at the work to be done and longs for a more glamorous life.

Many times we look at life and wish it could be changed. We may think how different things would have been for us if we had been born into a wealthy family. We may think how wonderful it would be if only God would, in some miraculous way, give us the things we dream of possessing.

What we do not realize is that God has already given us the things we dream of possessing, for

God has given us all good. We are inheritors of heaven. But what God gives us is in the realm of ideas, in the realm of Spirit.

God works through us. God needs our conscious cooperation; God needs our willing and alert minds; God needs our busy hands; God needs our constructive, productive efforts. God, working through us, brings forth His kingdom. God, working through us, is the transforming power that remakes and revitalizes our lives.

It is the very nature of us all to feel restless and dissatisfied with ourselves and our lives until we discover our spiritual selves, until we come to know, to feel, to experience unity with our Creator.

When we lift up our thinking, when we look for deeper meanings, when we open ourselves unreservedly to light and understanding, we discover that we do indeed live in the immediacy of God's presence, that we are not, never have been, and never will be separated from infinite love, infinite goodness, infinite life, and infinite power.

It takes practice, but anyone can learn to live with a continual sense of the immediacy of God's presence. No matter what the situation, no matter what the stress or strain, no matter what the demands made upon us, we can be calm, sure, trusting. We can be overcomers because we know that we are one with God.

Affirmations of Truth remind us that we are one with God—God who is harmony and order, the governing power of our minds, bodies, and affairs, the supply of our every need.

It is not always necessary to memorize an affirmation of Truth word-for-word. What is important is that the idea behind the affirmation become real and alive to you. This is how changes are wrought through affirmations: the words are translated into living Truth through the living faith of those who think on them, meditate on them, incorporate them into their very being.

It is a turning point for us when we realize the wonderful power and potential within us.

Not What You Want but What You Have

All of us have needs and longings, wants and desires. Most of us look to God, pray to God to help us satisfy our needs. But what most of us do not realize is that the needs, the longings, the wants, the desires, are not something that God will fulfill because we pray but something that God has already fulfilled before we ask, before we pray.

God has already answered our prayer; the need is already met. When we realize this, our prayer goes beyond asking or pleading. It becomes an affirmation of faith; it becomes a prayer of thankfulness for that which is even now ours in Spirit.

If there is lack in our lives, if we find ourselves in need of many things—a job, a home, money with which to meet bills—we may feel that we have good reason for worry and anxiety; we do not see where the money is coming from; we do not see how our needs are to be met.

Jesus said: *"Therefore I tell you, do not be anxious about your life, what you shall eat or what you shall drink, nor about your body, what you shall put on. Is not life more than food, and the body more than clothing? . . . your heavenly Father knows that you need them all. But seek first his kingdom and his righteousness, and all these things shall be yours as well."* (Matt. 6:25, 32-33)

To seek the kingdom first is to reverse our trend of thought from concentration on what we need and want to the realization of what we are and have.

It has been truly said that life is consciousness. What we are aware of, what we are conscious of, determines the kind of experiences we have. In order to rise out of want or lack we need to develop a "have" consciousness, rather than to stay in a "want" consciousness.

It comes as a jolting revelation to most persons to realize that they are what stands between them and their good. We are prone to blame conditions and circumstances; we feel that other persons have had opportunities we have not had. We are prone to believe that we are limited and held back, to think that if only we had great sums of money we could solve all our problems. But in this kind of thinking we are giving power to things; we are denying the power of God.

The "have" consciousness begins with the realization that we are children of God, that we have come into the world endowed with power and potential that are to be expressed and used, that the riches we discover are the inner riches of Spirit.

Jesus does not say that to seek the kingdom of God and His righteousness is to be poor, to do without the necessities of life. He says, in effect: "You are to put things in their right relationship. You are to realize that food and clothing and all the outer things are not the goal, the aim, the essence of life. When you place your faith in God, when you seek to express His Spirit, to fulfill His will and purpose, the things take care of themselves. Of course you will be fed; of course you will be clothed; of course you will be sheltered. This is part of God's love and provision and care.''

The New English Bible translates the verse, ''. . . *seek first his kingdom and his righteousness, and all these things shall be yours as well,*'' as ''Set your mind on God's kingdom and his justice before everything else, and all the rest will come to you as well.''

What we set our minds on before everything else determines what we have, what we are, what we experience. When Paul said that we should pray without ceasing, surely he meant that before everything else our minds should be set on God. When we are in need or want, before everything else let us set our minds on God, on His kingdom of good, on His justice. Let us declare in the face of need that we have the kingdom of God within us, that we have God on our side, that we have His law of love upon which to rely.

Not what we want in an outer way but what we have in our spiritual nature brings forth our own, establishes us forever in our good, assures us of abundance.

I inherit bountiful supply from God, my Father. All that He has is mine.

This is an affirmation of having, not a prayer of wanting or begging. We are children of a loving Father. His good is poured out without stint upon us. He says to us, "All that I have is yours." To know this is to have a rich consciousness, a feeling toward ourselves and life that is free and happy. God does not want us to be poor and inadequate. We are His children, heirs to all that He is. He has made us in His image. He expects us to be perfect, to show forth His greatness, His goodness, His power.

It is important to know what we want in life, but it is far more important to our success and prosperity to know what we already have. To seek and find the kingdom of God within us, to know ourselves as spiritual beings, is to discover our powers, our resources, to call forth that which we have from God.

V

A Turning Point:
When We Learn to Live Happily
with Ourselves and Others

Forgiveness—a Turning Point

To turn away from unforgiving thoughts and feelings, to be ready and willing to forgive and forget, can be a life-changing experience. Have you been carrying around with you some thought of unforgiveness toward someone or something?

You may be like the woman who said that she had hoarded old scars and hurts through the years. One day she read these words: "Let go of the past via forgiveness of self, others, circumstances."

She says that it sounded like such a simple step to take, yet somehow this idea had never been impressed on her in such a clear manner. She has a fresh outlook on this idea of forgiveness and is actively working on it, trying to release old hurts and even the memory of them.

A willingness to forgive and forget the past is a turning point that has nothing to do with how long one has lived. One comes to it whenever the light of understanding dawns in him.

When in the past you were hurt by someone, when you felt great waves of resentment and bitterness flow over you, did you feel close to God?

We separate ourselves from God and His love at the very time we need Him most, when we allow unhappy, unloving, hurt, unforgiving feelings to remain.

But you may say, "It is not all my fault; the other person is acting hatefully toward me, talking about me to others, refusing to speak to me," and so on. Even small children are not immune to such experiences and are made unhappy by them.

All of us accept the general idea of forgiveness, but only as we apply this forgiveness specifically in our own lives do we really know what it means and how freeing it is.

Suppose someone says that his problem may seem a minor one to others, but it has become a great source of worry and concern. This person has had a falling-out with a neighbor and the situation has continued so that now it is difficult to remember what the original quarrel was about. But the unhappy situation remains.

Obviously the one who would like to see the situation changed must be the one to set the law of divine love in motion.

How shall he begin?

Where shall he begin?

We always need to begin at the beginning, and the beginning of the solution to this particular problem is in the individual's own mind, reactions, and feelings.

It helps most of us to think of the person or the situation toward which we have felt unloving and unforgiving and to say definitely, specifically, "I forgive you."

Think of yourself as one with the great, over-shadowing love of God. See yourself and all persons, including the one you find it difficult to like, much less to love, as part of this divine love. Thinking of them in this way, you are able to say, "I love you, I bless you, I forgive you."

Those who have followed this practice have told us of many amazing things that followed. Like the walls of Jericho that needed only the right blasts of the trumpets to come tumbling down, so the walls of unforgiveness cannot withstand the right and powerful thought of love.

Others need your love and blessing, but you, more than anyone else, benefit from giving expression to forgiving love. This is the way of freedom and release. The binding thoughts are loosed, the tense muscles are relaxed, the taut emotions are quieted. Forgiving, you are forgiven. Blessing, you are blessed.

Recently a woman wrote to Unity saying that it was hard for her to ask God to forgive her when she could not forgive herself.

This is not an uncommon attitude. Most of those who feel that they cannot be forgiven for some past mistake are holding it so closely to themselves that they will not accept forgiveness. All the while they are carrying with them a weight of unforgiveness and a feeling of unworthiness, God has already forgiven them!

God's love is always poured out upon us, His forgiveness is always freely given; but we have to accept the idea of forgiveness and let the healing love of God fill our minds and hearts.

"If only I could relive some experience . . . ."

"If only I could let someone know I love him . . . ."

"If only it could have been different . . . ."

"If only I had not said the hurtful thing . . . ."

Let the "If onlys" go. Release them to God.

If ever we feel that we cannot forgive ourselves, let us know that God is not limited to our concept of forgiveness. What we cannot do, God can do. God loves us; God forgives us; God is with us to renew our spirits, to lift our hearts, to reveal a new way of life to us.

People sometimes ask how to handle the thoughts of regret and remorse over the past that rise unbidden to the mind. We may think that some incident has long since been forgotten, and then without conscious recall we are there again in thought, experiencing again some feeling of failure, hurt, or loss.

Sometimes we push back and repress feelings of guilt and self-condemnation; we relegate them to some dark corner of our minds. If we do this, such feelings are likely to rise up at unexpected moments. When this happens, as it does to most of us, it is helpful to think of such thoughts and feelings as rising to the surface of our minds in order to be redeemed and healed. We redeem them by realizing that the forgiving love of Jesus Christ penetrates to the depths of our being and sets us free from the mistakes of the past and the results of the mistakes of the past.

An affirmation such as: *The forgiving love of Jesus Christ penetrates to the depths of my being and sets me free* is powerful to set us free from anything we are holding, consciously or unconsciously, that needs to be forgiven.

"If the Son makes you free, you will be free indeed." (John 8:36) The forgiving love of Jesus Christ in us is able to eradicate buried guilt or resentment.

Through the forgiving love of Christ, we can let go of the past; we can forgive others; we can forgive ourselves. We can begin again, where we are, to express all that we long to express, to be all that we long to be.

Upon His Shoulders

The person who "blows his top," who takes out his anger and frustration on the people around him may think that he cannot help himself, that he is high-strung and nervous, that it is impossible for him to meet things calmly. If he tries, through dint of sheer willpower, to control his moods and disposition, he is not likely to succeed; he may find himself under more tension and stress than before.

Jesus said: *"I can do nothing on my own author-ity; . . . I seek not my own will but the will of him who sent me."* (John 5:30)

Anyone who finds it difficult to control his emo-tions needs to let go and let God work through him. When we do this we take a most necessary and important step toward the self-control we are seek-ing, for self-control comes as we are willing to let go of the drives, the desires, the demands of self, and let God take over in us.

The truly free and happy person is governed by the Spirit of God in him. He places himself, his affairs, his mind, his body in God's care and trusts implicitly in the power of God in him.

We overcome anxiety, tension, fearfulness through faith. Why are we ever anxious or upset? Only because we have allowed ourselves to become separated from God in our thought. We are work-ing and striving from personal consciousness only, and we think we have to do everything alone, that the burden of our life is on our shoulders only. We sometimes do not feel equal to the demands of life and so we meet life explosively rather than with faith and quiet confidence.

The beautiful prophecy in Isaiah concerning the

coming of Christ into the world is also a prophecy
concerning the coming of Christ in our lives, into
our thoughts, into our world.

> *And the government will be upon his shoulder,*
>   *and his name will be called*
> *"Wonderful Counselor, Mighty God,*
>   *Everlasting Father, Prince of Peace."*

(Isa. 9:6)

The government of your life will be upon His
shoulder. Think what this means. It means that
you are to trust the governing of all of your affairs,
the governing of your life, to the Christ. What kind
of a ruler is Christ? What kind of king is He?
. . . *His name will be called "Wonderful Counselor . . . Prince of Peace."* Think of the wonderful Spirit of Christ as ruling and reigning in you.
Think of the Counselor who is all justice, all might,
all Truth as being in you, as ruling and governing
your thoughts, your life and affairs. The government of your life rests securely upon the shoulder
of almighty God, the everlasting Father. The
government of your emotions is given over to the
direction of the loving Christ, the Prince of Peace.

Every time you are tempted to feel worried or
upset, remind yourself that God is the governing
power in your life. Say to yourself: *I place myself*

and all my affairs upon His shoulder. I trust God to bless, to guide, to direct, to govern all that concerns me. I relax and rest in the faith that all is well.

When we follow Jesus in knowing that we can of ourselves do nothing, we need to follow Him in knowing that through the power of God in us we can do all things. Not of ourselves, but in and through God's power in us are we able to surmount and surpass what seem to be problems or obstacles. With humans many things seem impossible, but with God all things are possible.

Often we feel defeated and frustrated not because of our inability to accomplish but because we procrastinate. We do not arouse to action, we do not use the powers and abilities that are in us. When we put off our good, making excuses to ourselves and others for not doing the things we know we should do, we need to put a new spirit into our thinking. We need to enliven the inner self. We need to let go of the old, limited way of thinking and proclaim the power of God that is in us, to rely on this power, to let His Spirit, His will, govern and direct us, inspire and quicken us.

Have You Tried Blessing It?

If you have some problem facing you, if there is some unfulfilled longing in your heart, if there is some urgent need in your life, have you tried blessing it?

If you are having difficulty getting along with some other person, have you tried blessing him?

If your need is health, have you tried blessing your body?

If your need is supply, have you tried blessing your affairs?

What does it mean to bless a problem, a need, a situation? To bless it is to quit fighting it. Perhaps this is the meaning, in part at least, of Jesus' words: *Agree with thine adversary quickly . . . .* (Matt. 5:25 A.V.) To bless anything is to agree with it spiritually, to see God, to see the good, where before you have seen something disturbing, troubling, or hurtful.

When we bless the troublesome situation, the unhappy environment, the unhealthy body, the appearance of lack or failure, this does not mean that we are resigning ourselves to it but rather that we are letting go of our fear, our anxiety about ourselves or anyone else; that we are <u>beholding the</u> <u>good which is always present,</u> that we are remembering the loving presence of God which pervades and permeates all.

<u>When we bless our problems, a change always</u> <u>takes place, but the first and greatest change that</u> <u>takes place is within us.</u>

We cannot say, "I bless this situation (or this person or this need); I behold the goodness of God at work," and still feel fearful. The word of blessing invokes God's power in us and a change is wrought in our thinking and feeling. Then our words of blessing carry weight and spiritual power as we pour them forth on conditions, situations, and persons.

Sometimes we are asked, "Just how do you go about blessing something that so far has seemed to resist prayers, tears, and everything else?"

Let us suppose that, for example, you are worried about your affairs. Your finances seem to be in a muddle; you have obligations that seem beyond your capacity to meet; you are so worried that your worry is affecting your work. You are finding it difficult to concentrate; you find yourself cross and irritable with your family and those with whom you work. You feel separated from God's help and

love. You pray, you lie awake night after night worrying. You arise tired and tense, almost afraid to face another day.

Then someone tells you about this idea of blessing and you decide to try it. So you start with what seems to be worrying you most—your finances—and you bless them. You give thanks that God is your supply. You bless your mind; you bless it for its ability to use wisdom and good judgment in handling your money and affairs.

Then you bless your environment, your family; you let go of unhappy or quarrelsome thoughts. You bless everything and everyone around you and behold the goodness of God at work. You place your blessing upon your work, your coworkers. You change your thoughts from a state of irritability to one of confidence and peace. You bless your mind, your heart, your hands.

When you consciously take time to bless yourself, your life, your affairs, to bless all the persons about you, you not only help to establish a more peaceful state of mind in yourself, you actually invoke a power for good that begins its work and brings forth results—results that are sometimes astonishing.

There is great power in blessing, for when we

when we

bless we express divine love and call it to life in us, in all that concerns us. Nothing in the world is more powerful than divine love; nothing is more magnetic in its drawing power; nothing changes and transforms as wholly and completely as does the word of blessing, spoken in love, sent forth on wings of divine love.

Think of the power of blessing. Bless your substance, bless your affairs, bless the power of divine love at work in you. Give thanks that you are a child of God, that His love provides for your every need, that His substance is with you eternally, that in Him you are continually blessed.

One Thing Is Needful

A friend once said, "We've had a terrible time at our house this morning, all on account of me!" She went on to say that always before she had blamed others for inharmony and confusion, but on this particular morning it had been revealed to her in a flash of insight that she was the storm center, that she was the troublemaker. She wanted now to express the Christ love so that she might be

a peacemaker, so that she might promote understanding and harmony.

Each of us has the capacity in us to rise out of
critical and faultfinding ways. We have the capacity
to express the self we long to express. Sometimes it
may seem that the more we determine to be loving,
understanding, uncritical, the harder it is. Regard-
less of our firm resolve, we find ourselves disturbed
and upset; we hear ourselves voicing criticism and
complaint. One woman said she would find it easy
to be a good Truth student if it were not for her
family!

When we are unhappy and dissatisfied with the
people around us, when we see their faults, when
we are annoyed or irritated by the way they do or
do not do things, we need to take our eyes off of
others and look to our self, for such feelings reveal a
basic dissatisfaction with our self. Sometimes we do
not like our self at all, and we project these feelings
to others. We transfer the blame for the way we feel
from our self to the other person.

When we feel right and at peace within, we find
it much easier to accept and approve of others,
much easier to love and understand them. If we are
unhappy in our home or if any human relationship
is a source of distress to us, we need to take our

attention away from the inharmony and turn to God, to open up to His Spirit, to open our minds to His light, to open our hearts to His love.

Jesus said: *"You, therefore, must be perfect, as your heavenly Father is perfect."* (Matt. 5:48) This is our concern—to put on the perfection in which we are created. What makes us unhappy is trying to make others conform to our idea of perfection. We find it impossible to conform to our human idea of perfection. The perfection we want, the perfection that is possible, is the perfection of Spirit. The perfectionist may be a most difficult person to live with. The person who is striving to follow the perfect Christ Way is filled with a spirit of love and joy; he radiates peace, he blesses everyone around him.

Mary and Martha illustrate the two sides of our nature. The Martha side, the perfectionist, is so occupied with the things of the outer, so desirous that no one shall be able to find fault with us, that sometimes, like Martha, we cannot even stop to listen to our indwelling Lord. Jesus lovingly reminded Martha: *". . . you are anxious and troubled about many things; one thing is needful. Mary has chosen the good portion . . . ."* (Luke 10:41-42)

When we find ourselves feeling overburdened by many duties and cares, when it seems that we are the only one really concerned about things, that others leave all the work to us while they enjoy life, we should stop and remember that but one thing is needful, to express the Christ, to let His power and love flow through us. If we think that we are doing everything, without credit or appreciation, then we may be sure that we are working in personal consciousness. We are not letting God work through us. We need to return to God in quiet prayer, to get back on a spiritual level. When we do this, it is surprising how our attitude changes. We still are able to accomplish a great deal, but with a feeling of freedom and ease. And no longer are we filled with resentment or criticism because of what another does or does not do. We see all other persons with the vision of the Christ; we bless them, inspire them, and encourage them by our faith.

We do not have to belabor ourselves for past mistakes or past failures. But one thing is needed; to let the Christ love flow forth through us. This love is already within us. We need only to let it flow forth to discover how healing it is, how quickly it dissolves discord, how forgiving its nature, how transforming its power.

VI

A Turning Point:
When We Voice Our Thanks

Go Your Way Rejoicing

There are some people who equate religion with a long face, with suffering and sorrow. They believe that they cannot be happy and lighthearted and still serve God.

Nothing could be further from the truth! The Bible is filled with songs of praise, with words of joy and rejoicing. "Cruden's Complete Concordance" lists 236 references to *rejoice* and *rejoicing*, whereas *sad, sorrowful, fearful, troubled* all combined are referred to less than a hundred times.

Sometimes we let ourselves believe that God wants us to suffer, that if we are truly good we will have so much to bear that we cannot be happy or carefree. If we do not have troubles of our own, then we take on the troubles of other persons.

Charles Fillmore used to tell about the woman who said, "When the Lord sends tribulations, I tribulate!"

There are times in our lives when we have something difficult to meet and we feel heavy-hearted. But everyone has had the experience at some time of releasing his problem or need to God—really releasing it—and feeling a great wave of rejoicing filling him. The need was still there, the problem was still there, but the person knew, with a knowing that was beyond reason or explanation, that God was with him, that God would see him through. Heaviness of heart was transformed into a feeling of joy.

We may think that if everything were perfect in our lives, we could rejoice. Surprisingly sometimes, we discover that in the darkest night our hearts still sing their songs of rejoicing.

It is our very nature as spiritual beings to rejoice, to feel joy, to feel delight in life and living. We do not feel more spiritual because we are serious and sad. We feel the closest to God when we feel joyful, when in our inner selves we sing for joy and dance for gladness.

Even when we feel down, when everything in life looks bleak and dark, still the lifting Spirit of

Christ is in us and will break through and shine forth like the morning sun.

Lowell Fillmore once told about a man who came to him for help and counsel. No matter what Lowell said to him, the man remained sunk in depression. There was no answering light in his eyes to the words of Truth that Lowell spoke to him, there was no lift to the shoulders; there was no response, only despair.

Lowell finally said, "Well, you know, it's always darkest before the dawn." The shoulders straightened up, the eyes lighted up, the man jumped up and said, "That's what I've been waiting to hear!" So sometimes even the trite saying comes to life and has meaning when it strikes a responsive chord in us, when something in us rises up in faith and brings us to our feet again, spiritually and physically.

Joy is not something we feel because something happens to make us glad. Joy is an inner quality that is always there.

Joy is a gift from God, as much a part of our makeup, as much a part of our nature, as life itself. It is our nature to be joyous, to be filled with an inner feeling of gladness and rejoicing.

Does it seem to you that some people are naturally joyful, that they have inner springs of joy that sustain them?

You may not think that you, too, have inner springs of joy, but you do. Joy is an inherent God-quality in you that is fed and nourished by the Spirit of God in you. You may repress this joy, you may keep it dammed up by unhappy, depressed thinking, but it wells up often enough, unexpectedly enough, for you to be aware of it.

How can you be more joyous? How can you release the God-given joy that is within you?

Just to think about the joy as being within you, to think of it as a wellspring within you, fed continually by the Spirit, helps you to become more aware of joy, more open to it, more expressive of it.

The surest, truest way to find joy is to find God within yourself, to be aware of His presence, to have a sense of His power. To know that you are one with God is to have an abiding reason for joy, joy that nothing can take away.

Sometimes people are amazed to discover that in their most serious moments, times when they are striving most earnestly to lift up their thoughts and hearts to God, joy wells up and seems to overflow in them. They are surprised by this upwelling joy because they have expected prayer to be arduous.

They may have begun their prayer with a heavy heart, with a mind weighted down with care. Then, suddenly, they are light and free and joyous! Whenever we are close to God, one with Him, we feel glowing joy, radiant joy.

The more you let the joy of the Lord fill you, flow through you, the easier you find it is to live your life successfully, wisely, productively.

When joy is released in us, we are set free from depressing, heavy thoughts and emotional states that make us feel it is no use trying. The freeing joy that springs up in us from God gives wings to our spirit and makes everything easier, happier, and more nearly perfect for us.

You can refuse to let any kind of negative thoughts and feelings remain with you; you can learn to keep your heart tuned in to joy; you can learn to listen to the joyous song of your inmost being.

Mental depression can retard healing, as we all know. Our body is a responsive instrument, and when we are sad, unhappy, or fearful, we make it harder for the body to lay hold of the healing power of God. When we are in need of healing, let us pray not only for the body, but for the mind and spirit as well. Let us know that healing is taking place in us, first of all as a quickening of faith in us, as a breaking through of light in us, as a rising up in us of the indomitable Spirit of God that has been with us from the beginning.

As we practice relaxing and letting go and resting in the healing life and love of God, we shall find that we do not have to work to lift up our spirits, for our natural good spirits will reassert themselves; the faith that is in us will reassert itself; and we will be sustained by a feeling of inner joy that God alone can give.

No matter what is before you now, God is within you. You have the power and the ability to meet all things. Knowing this, you can go your way rejoicing.

If you have some decision facing you and you cannot seem to resolve it, place it in God's care. Affirm right now that God's light and intelligence are shining in you, showing you the way, guiding you to make the right decision. Then let the matter rest, and go your way rejoicing.

If you are troubled and unhappy because of the need of some dear one, place this dear one in God's care. You cannot live his life for him, but you can know that he has God's Spirit within him to guide him. Let the matter rest. Release your anxiety and concern, and go your way rejoicing.

If you find it hard to be happy because of feelings of envy or jealousy of other persons who seem to have more, to be more than you, take this need to Spirit. What such feelings are trying to tell you is that you have capacities within yourself that need expressing. Listen to the Spirit of God in you that inspires you to be more, to do more, to give more, to live more. Release envy and jealousy. Walk with confidence in your own divine Self, and go your way rejoicing.

If you are unhappy, disappointed in love, if you feel let down by some person, say to yourself: *God means happiness for me. No one or no thing can take away my joy or peace of mind. I release all thoughts of bitterness. I open my heart and mind and life to new and happy experiences.* Then let the matter rest, and go your way rejoicing.

If yours is a health need and you have prayed and prayed without the hoped-for results, release your concern over your health to God. Let His healing work be done in you. Affirm: *Thank You, God, for healing me now.* Then let the matter rest, and go your way rejoicing.

If you have a need for supply of some kind—a job, a home, money to pay bills—and your peace of mind is disturbed by your worry and anxiety, give the need over to God. Know that God is your unfailing resource. Know that in Him every need is perfectly met. Give thanks for supply, here and now. Then let the matter rest, and go your way rejoicing.

This inner feeling of joy and great delight, this spirit of rejoicing, is not something you have to create, to put on. It would be impossible to do so. Rather, it is a feeling you open yourself to and let come through. It is a feeling that is already a part of you. Just as a small child expresses joy easily and naturally, so can you. This spirit can become suppressed by layers of fears and tears and years.

But it is there! Let it well up! Let it find expression! Go your way rejoicing!

Thankfulness Is More than Saying ''Thank You''

Suppose someone were to say to you, ''You should be very thankful for all your blessings.'' You would no doubt agree, but you would not necessarily *feel* thankful.

We are not thankful because we should be or because it is our duty. We are not thankful because, by presidential proclamation, a day is set aside as Thanksgiving Day. We are not thankful because we are told to be thankful. Why are we thankful?

Thankfulness is more than just saying "thank you," although some of us need to voice our thanks more than we do. A person may feel very thankful but never express this thankful feeling in words. How good it is to voice our thanks, to say "thank you" to another person, to say "thank you" to God.

But thankfulness is more than this. It is an attitude, a feeling of appreciation. It is our whole approach to life.

Do we say "thank you" to the towering majesty of mountains, to a glorious spring day, to a tree ablaze with fall colors? Do we say "thank you" to the perfect rose in our garden? Perhaps not in so many words, but our awareness of beauty, our enjoyment of life, our appreciation of persons, places, and things—these are ways in which we express our thankfulness.

Do we say "thank you" to the members of our family for being there when we need them, for the things they do for us? Do we thank our children for the joy they bring to us? Do we say "thank you" to our friends for the ways in which they share in our lives and interests? Not in so many words, as a rule—but our love for our family, our dear ones, our appreciation of our friends, all are a way of expressing our thankfulness.

Every time we turn to God in thought, in prayer, in meditation, we may not say, "Thank You, God," in so many words, but our feeling of oneness with God and His good, our awareness of His great love and all-enfolding care—this is a way of saying "thank You," this feeling of thankfulness welling up within us.

The thankful spirit is like the loving heart; it is ours because of the way we feel and respond to life. No one can command us to have a loving heart. No one can command us to have a thankful spirit. This is the inner realm where we have dominion.

No one person has more capacity for thankfulness than another; he has just awakened more of a responsive spirit. The thankful spirit is in all of us. It is irrepressible. Even a person who is downhearted and depressed can be quickly lifted to a feeling of thankfulness by a word of praise, by some evidence that God loves him, by even some slight indication that the world is good, that he is important and needed by others.

The very nature of our being is to be thankful. If we could hear them, it is likely that the very cells of our body sing for joy.

Why is the Bible so filled with words of praise and thanksgiving; why are the Psalms such songs of joy? Because it is man's nature to pour out his heart in thanks. It is the nature of man to rejoice in life.

When we do not feel thankful, we do not really feel alive. When we do not feel thankful, we do not feel right within. We feel that something is lacking. And indeed it is. What is lacking is our release of the thankful spirit that is in us, the spirit that is waiting to rise up in wonder and awe, the spirit that sees life and all of life as great and good and remarkable.

We have heard it said of some person that he is most ungrateful, that he takes everything for granted, that he never expresses a word of appreciation. Perhaps if we could see inside the heart and mind of such a person, we would discover that his real lack is the ability to let himself feel alive and grateful. His real lack is not lack of appreciation but lack of practice in expressing his true feelings.

There is not a person who does not have an instinct for thanksgiving, not one of us who does not have a soul that relates to his Creator, a soul that cries out in the depths of us, "How good, how great Thou art!" This feeling may be so submerged that we do not know it is there. Certainly we do not always hear it or express it. But some time, somewhere along the way, something stirs us to a feeling of such awe and thankfulness that in the secret place of our soul, we drop to our knees as it were, and say, "Thank You, God! Thank you, life!"

If ever we feel that life has gone flat or stale, the fault may not lie with life. Life may seem to be lacking in zest because we have become so engrossed in everyday living that we have fallen into a take-it-for-granted attitude.

We all have had the experience of seeming suddenly to come alive. The world that looked so commonplace and ordinary took on a sheen and a glory. The people whom we had come to think of as ordinary, even dull, seemed remarkable. What changed? What made this transformation? Through some tiny crack of light in our soul a spark of thankfulness had escaped.

Even this small ray of thankfulness cast its glow. We thought about some person, perhaps the one at the desk next to ours, and saw him as though for the first time. We said to ourselves, "How fine he is!'' We thought about some event or situation that did not seem out of the ordinary before, and we thought: How remarkable it all is! How fortunate I am! How good God is!

This is the true spirit of thanksgiving that cannot be confined to one day of the year, the spirit of thanksgiving that wells up at the most unexpected times, the spirit of thanksgiving in us that has its song to sing, and will sing it—sometimes in spite of us!

Let us be thankful for our thankful spirit, the spirit that God created in us, the spirit that lends enchantment and excitement and wonder to life. This spirit of thankfulness is there. Let us give it voice!

VII

A Turning Point:
When We Know What to Remember
and What to Forget

Thanks for the Memories!

A few memories stay with us forever and become a part of the eternal. Most of the events of our lives are transitory, passing. They come "to pass," not to be remembered or dwelt on.

There are persons who have been in perilous situations, when it seemed that they could not survive, who have reported that at the time their whole life passed before their eyes.

This is not the way most of us remember our lives. They do not come to mind in chronological order or as a series of connected happenings. But we remember in bits and pieces, in flashbacks. We may remember something from earliest childhood that it would seem we could not possibly remember. It may be only a fleeting memory, but it has stayed with us through the years.

Sometimes, something that someone says today, or hearing someone whistle a few bars of a song, or driving into a sunset, we have a flash of memory of something totally unrelated to what is happening now, but somehow called up by it and somehow related to it.

Perhaps this is because our growing is not a matter of birthdays, not a matter of graduating from school, or gaining success in a job. Our growing is a matter of coming to understand ourselves and others and God. Whether we remember something that happened ten years ago, or fifty, or yesterday, is not too important. That we remember forever those times when light broke through, those times when we truly felt our oneness with God, those times when we put aside fear and selfishness and acted with love and compassion—this kind of re-membering gives beauty and depth and color to our living.

What do we remember? The memory that has meaning for us is not the memory of an event but of a feeling, an emotion. Poetry is memory dis-tilled. Writing is memory set down in words. History is memory teaching us something today. Biography is memory shared.

To remember can be good, but also, to remember can be not good. We need to remember; we need to forget. How we remember and how we forget—this is the key.

A person who has been hurt or humiliated may live with the unpleasant memory; he keeps bringing it up in his mind long after the incident is over. This is negative remembering. This calls for forgiveness. This person does not need God's forgiveness; he already has it. He needs to forgive himself, to forgive everyone and everything that his mind has held to, has carried as remembered hurt. Then he needs to know that he is free from even the memory of hurt feelings or pride. He can close that door forever. But in forgetting deliberately, in erasing the unhappy memory through letting the forgiving love of God fill him and heal him of all past hurts, he is creating a memory to cherish. Now when he looks back on that time, he will not remember the hurt; he will remember the healing love of God that took over, and this will be a memory to bless.

One woman described herself as a worrier. She was fearful and negative, expecting the worst. She had a bad childhood and many years of strife, many times her life was in danger, and she didn't know how to express love and affection. But someone gave her *DAILY WORD* and she began to apply the ideas to her thinking. She has never before felt so free and serene. The old memories of unhappiness are fading; she is remembering the truth that God loves her, and her life is changing.

Another friend told of the wonderful change that has taken place in her way of thinking, in the way she is able to meet problems and assume a happy, positive attitude toward life. She was fired from her job, and her whole world seemed to fall apart. She went home in despair, and her attention focused on these lines from a prayer she had on her bedroom wall: "Whether or not it is clear to you, no doubt the universe is unfolding as it should." These words gave her new hope. She realized that she had not been happy in her work; she could see that, with the experience gained, she was better prepared for whatever else might come. This flash of inspiration and insight enabled her to set her course. She decided not only to ask God for guidance but to listen. She determined that she would not worry about finances and that she would spend much time in study, prayer, and meditation. She says that at what had been one of the lowest times of her life, her spirits soared! Needless to say she now has a better job and is finding life increasingly happy every day. I do not think she will remember much about the lost job; I believe she will never forget the help that came from the presence of God within her, when she needed it!

What kind of memories are we to cherish, to give thanks for?

None of us should spend our time and thought in thinking of the past, however wonderful, in talking about and remembering other times, other persons, other places, in sighing for days that are no more. The truly alive person, whatever his age— nineteen or ninety—never does this. He or she is too interested in the present, in what is happening around him or her, in meeting the demands and the joys of today.

But the memories we have of times when we stood fast in faith, the memories we have of healing taking place, the memories we have of feeling God's presence and power in a time of need, the memories we have of being comforted and upheld in a time of bereavement—these memories do not pull us backward but help us to meet today and its needs a little better, with a little more courage and strength.

In good times and in bad times, in happy times,

in sad times, we have been role players, observers, listeners, learners. The memories we give thanks for are the experiences that have given us insight and understanding; the experiences that have brought us closer to God; the experiences that have demanded much of us and brought out qualities and capacities that we did not know we possessed.

The memories that are always alive and fresh and are a part of today are the memories of emotion, faith, and feeling.

They are the memory of a word spoken that changed our lives.

They are the memory of a hand outstretched that made us know that we were loved.

They are the memory of those times when we suddenly knew and felt and stood in the presence of God.

They are the memory of understanding breaking like sunlight into our minds.

They are the memory of grief being transformed into faith, yes, joy!

So, thanks for the memories!

He Is Not Here

Why seek ye the living among the dead? He is not here, but is risen . . . . (Luke 24:5, 6 A.V.) How many of us seek the living among the dead— the faded hopes, the unfulfilled dreams, the lost yesterdays!

Sometimes without our conscious realization of it, our thoughts, faith, and interest are centered in the past. We go over and over the experiences of the past. We talk about other times, other places, other persons, and lose our living hold on the present.

Sometimes we think that if we could go back to the way things once were, we would be happy. But anyone who attempts to reenter the past is sure to be disappointed. Anyone who has ever revisited the place of his birth after years of absence is shocked by the difference between the way the place actually is and the way he remembered it. He may walk along the old familiar streets, but he is a stranger in a strange land. He has thought of this place as his home, but he finds that he is no longer here even in spirit. He has gone on into a new and different life, and in thinking longingly of the past he has given his thought and interest to something that no longer exists.

Not every person carries pleasant memories of the past in his heart—to some the past is an unwelcome intruder on present joys, bringing a continual reminder of the times they failed, of the persons and circumstances that disappointed them, of the unhappiness they experienced, of the injustices they suffered. They cannot disassociate themselves from past failures and disappointments, even though they have long since risen above them, even though they are far different now than they were in the past.

Every time we come through an experience we gain understanding, we grow and learn. Because we were once afraid, because we were once immature in our approach to life, because we were once lacking in faith and courage is no reason we should continue to think of ourselves in this light today.

The spirit in us that is God's own Spirit continually impels us to new heights, continually says to the self of us that would look to the past with either longing or regret, *He is not here, but is risen . . . .*

Sometimes we think of ourselves as being in bondage to some habit, to some person, or to some circumstance. We might feel we are unable to free ourselves, we think of ourselves as weak, as lacking in willpower, while all the time our freedom is close at hand.

The beginning of freedom lies in a spiritual awakening. Whenever we begin to think of ourselves as spiritual beings, whenever we begin to think of the Spirit of God in us as always present, as all-powerful, as stronger than any human weakness or bondage, we rise to a new place in consciousness, and go through a spiritual resurrection.

Sometimes it is not we who are bound but we who try to bind others to us. Often we bind those we love in our thought about them. We keep them bound to the past; we remember them as they were rather than realizing that they, too, are growing and continually rising to a new place in consciousness. We bind those we love because we are not willing for them to change.

Sometimes we are disappointed and hurt by our families and friends, because the close relationship we once enjoyed seems lost; we no longer have common interests, we no longer speak the same language. Love never changes, but we continually change and we must be willing to accept changes in ourselves and in others; we must be willing to go forward in faith, to establish new bonds of love and friendship, to have a new vision, a new understanding of the persons about us. We need to be willing to let go of old memories of other persons, we need to free them in our thought about them, to cease remembering and talking about something they did or said years ago. Thus, shall we be able to see them as new persons, even as each of us may feel that we are new persons.

Sometimes it is difficult for parents to accept the growth and change that take place in their children. They may dread seeing the children grow up and take their place in life. But actually no parent wants his child to remain childish and dependent. When parents accept the changes that come in the development of their children, when they rejoice in all the ways that their children grow and unfold, even if it takes the children on paths that are opposite from their own, both they and the children are happier, and the bond between them remains strong through the years.

Rather than saying with despair that the child seems changed, they say with thankfulness, "He is not here, but is risen." They view the changes that take place in the child as good, as part of his growth and unfoldment; and more important, they keep faith in God's Spirit in the child, the Spirit that "will neither slumber nor sleep," that will guide and guard him, that will continually lift him up in mind, soul, and body.

True forgiveness rests on the idea that "He is not here, but is risen." As long as we think about the thing that needs to be forgiven, as long as we find it hard to forgive someone for the thing he did that hurt us or someone else, we are seeking the living among the dead. We shall not find forgiveness, peace of mind, or understanding in this way. But when we can lift up our thought, when we can say, "I forgive you," to the person or the situation that has made us unhappy, when we are able to say with understanding and compassion as did Jesus, "Father, forgive them; for they know not what they do," then we shall lay hold of the living idea of love. We shall no longer have anything to forgive, for love will wipe out even the memory of the hurt.

And love will help us to look on the person who has disappointed us or hurt us, and say with faith, "He is not here, but is risen." This is another way of saying, "I behold the Christ in you." When we free the other person in our thought about him, when we affirm that he has an uplifting, resurrecting Spirit in him, we are making great progress in our own spiritual overcoming as well as helping to uplift him. Jesus pointed out this truth when He said: "*. . . And I, when I am lifted up . . . will draw all men to myself.*" (John 12:32)

"*Why seek ye the living among the dead? He is not here, but is risen.*"

We cannot find faith, hope, love, and understanding somewhere in the past. We cannot find them by dwelling on the happiness of the past any more than we can find them by dwelling on the unpleasant things of the past. There is a spirit in each of us that is God's own Spirit. It is a renewing, resurrecting spirit. Whenever we feel low in spirit or despair because we cannot seem to meet the conditions in life happily and successfully, we need only to turn to Spirit in order to feel an uplift. We need only to trust this Spirit and we are able to turn to the present with new faith, we are able to let go of the past, we are able to say to the self of us that was bound or troubled in any way, "This is no longer true of me. I am not here, I am risen!"

Have You Forgotten Something?

Cross out the doubts of other years;
Cross out the hurts, the griefs, the fears.
Christ is your life, your light, your way.
Christ resurrects your soul today!

When I have something before me to do that necessitates remembering several things at one time, I often make a list, headed perhaps by the words "Things to Do." As these things are accomplished I cross them out. Certainly, I am not sad when I cross them out. Rather, it is with a sense of relief and achievement that I do it. It is a good feeling to know that I have done what needs to be done, that I have not left things at loose ends.

We can have this same kind of feeling about spiritual crossing out. When we think of something we need or want to overcome, we may feel heavy or depressed. Perhaps we have times when we long to be free from old fears and hurts and limitations, but we do not know how to go about it.

Why not approach it as practically and positively as we approach the accomplishment of some ordinary task? It might even be helpful to make a list of

"Things to Do" to set our minds, our thoughts, in the direction we want to go. Then the crossing out we do will not be negative renunciation but rather, positive, step-by-step overcoming. With each small gain we can shorten our list of "Things to Do" and add to our sense of accomplishment and fulfillment.

Are you fearful—fearful of the future, fearful of other persons, fearful of being alone? It does not matter what seems to be the reason for your fear, you can begin to cross it out by making a "Things to Do" list headed with something like this: *I have faith. I am not alone. God is with me at all times and in all places.*

For instance, when you have a shopping list it is necessary to look at it to remind yourself that you are not forgetting anything. Similarly, a spiritual reminder needs to be looked at, to be brought to mind.

If you are working to overcome fear and there are times when it seems to get the upper hand, ask yourself, "Have I forgotten something?" If you have made a "Things to Do" list, get it out, look at it, accept its reminder to have faith, to trust in God and His power within you. With or without such a list, the need is to remember what it is that you are to do, to remember that you are to have faith, and thus to cross out fear.

You are crossing out fear every time you let faith be your guide rather than fear—every time you say in your heart, "I will trust," rather than giving way to fear. Spiritual overcoming does not usually arrive in one grand leap forward, but rather is a process of unfoldment, thought by thought, experience by experience.

The reminder to have faith may be one that you need to put on your list of things to remember and to do, again and again. But every time you are able to follow through on this reminder and stand in faith, even if it is only in some small matter, you are on your way toward overcoming fear.

If you are easily upset, easily hurt, if it seems to you that other persons do not understand or appreciate you, your "Things to Do" list might carry a reminder such as this: *I will be a center of harmony and peace. I will let the love of God express itself through me.* The more you follow through on this affirmation, the more peaceful and harmonious you will feel; for the more you express God's love, the more you draw to yourself happy and loving experiences.

Sometimes we cannot feel loving toward someone who is hateful or hurtful. We may not love what a person says or does, but we can love the Christ in him, the Spirit of God in him. This is the way of understanding; this is the way of forgiveness; this is the way of releasing bitterness from our hearts; this is the way of pouring out a blessing of peace and love on others.

To be a little more loving, a little more understanding, a little more tolerant, a little more forgiving is to cross out the limitations in us; it is to free ourselves to live more joyously and effectively.

Whatever you would like to see healed or helped, whatever you would like to change or improve in your life, in whatever way you would like to overcome, think in terms of crossing it out spiritually. You can do all things through Christ who strengthens you. You can cross out the old ways, the old beliefs, the old you. And in this crossing out, Christ is resurrected in you as life in your body, as light in your mind, as love in your heart, as power in your life, as peace in your affairs.

Moments to Remember

I heard a friend describe a spring evening on a houseboat. She said it was a perfect evening—a full moon, and whippoorwills were calling across the water. If she were a poet, she would have written a poem about it. In trying to describe the exquisite beauty of the evening, she said, "It is something I will remember all my life!"

Another friend, who was retiring, was surrounded by friends at a luncheon in her honor. She had been given a most welcome gift of money for what she called her "moving fund." With shining eyes she said, "This is something I will never forget! I'll treasure this moment always."

I thought about how often we talk about letting go of the past, and we need to, of course. But part of what we are, what we become, is made up of those rare times when we experienced such joy, such peace, such appreciation, such an overwhelming sense of goodness and beauty that the moment became unforgettable.

Sometimes a person who is upset can find inner calm and peace more quickly if he quiets his thoughts, stills his body, and in his mind's eye pictures some remembered scene of beauty—perhaps a serene mountain lake, or a green country road, or it may be the memory of whippoorwills calling across a lake at dusk.

Somewhere deep within we all have memories of a moment when we felt truly loved and appreciated, memories of a moment when we were understood, memories of an unforgettable word spoken to us. These are moments that the heart stores up, moments that make us feel warmed by God's love, and comforted.

A friend told me about the time he wrote a brief note of appreciation to a man, a musician, who had been before the public for years. No doubt this man had heard many words of praise for his work. But this brief note touched him deeply and became one of his unforgettable memories. His secretary said that he had had it framed and kept it on his desk.

We may have added a treasured moment to someone's memories without being aware of it. Certainly, there are those whom we will remember always for some word they said, for some kindness they offered.

Remembered moments of beauty, remembered moments of someone's caring and sharing, these increase our ability to appreciate the present and to express our love and appreciation.

VIII

A Turning Point:
When We Do Not Give Up
or Give in to Fear

Perfect Love Casts out Fear

The greatest need for freedom is freedom from fear. <u>It is fear that keeps us from experiencing the joy and happiness that life has to offer us.</u>

What are we afraid of? Are we afraid that some harm will befall us? . . . *Perfect love casts out fear.* . . . (I John 4:18) When we know that we are beloved of God, that He is always with us, we go our way secure and unafraid. In unfamiliar places, walking, riding, flying, we can feel so enfolded in the love of God that we are free from fear.

Are we afraid of other people? Do we fear their opinion of us? Do we fear that someone can keep our good from us? Perfect love casts out fear. We overcome our fear of people as we let love fill our hearts, as we know that God is love and that in His love we are one with all people. If we can encircle the one we fear with our loving prayers, we will find ourselves free, completely free, of fear.

Are we afraid of our own inadequacy? Are we afraid of failure or defeat? Perfect love casts out fear. Such fear begins in our own minds, and such fear can be overcome in our own minds. As we think of ourselves as spiritual beings, beloved of God, we no longer belittle ourselves, we no longer think in terms of frustration and failure. Perfect love, the love of God in us, fills us with self-assurance and emboldens us to try the thing we have feared, to attempt the thing we have longed to do or be but have held back from in fear. Perfect love assures us that through the power of God within us we have nothing to fear. In Him we are more than adequate; we are capable of victorious, triumphant expression.

Are we afraid of disease or ill health? Perfect love casts out fear. Perfect love, God's love, is a healing force, and his love is within us. This love is mighty to free us from fear and to heal us. We do not fear any condition, for we know that God is the life within us, that with Him all things are possible. We are free, free to accept life and health, free to be renewed and restored.

Are we afraid of lack? <u>Perfect love casts out fear.</u> <u>In God, in His perfect love, there is unlimited</u> <u>supply. His perfect love provides the substance out</u> <u>of which all things come.</u> Do we look at our income and fear that it will not be enough to meet our needs? <u>Let us eliminate fear by blessing our supply,</u> <u>by seeing all our supply as an outpouring of God's</u> <u>love. There are no shortages in God; there is no</u> <u>lack in God. Always His abundance pours forth.</u> Fear will not block our way nor keep us from experiencing God's abundance, as we banish fear with faith in the love, the all-providing love of God.

Are we afraid of the future? Do we dread the passing of years? Perfect love casts out fear. The future will become the now, and today and in the days to come, God is with us, His love is with us. Fear of the future cannot remain with us as we live today, this very minute, conscious of God's love, grateful for God's love. He is with us. What is there to fear?

Are we afraid to be alone? Perfect love casts out fear. Perfect love, God's love, gives us the assurance that we are never alone. Wherever we are, God is; we are always one with Him. <u>The love of</u> <u>God transforms loneliness into happiness and new-</u>

ness of living as we know that we are not alone, that God loves us and guides us and shows us how to enlarge the scope of our lives, how to welcome new relationships, how to express more of the love of God so that we are loving channels for the help and comfort of others.

Do Not Give Up

What are your longings? What are your dreams? What are your desires?

Do not give up trying to make them a reality. Do not let yourself believe that their fulfillment is impossible to you.

Have courage. Press forward with confidence. Know that God is within you, that His wisdom is guiding you.

If your life seems difficult, if it seems that troubles mount instead of abating, say to yourself, "Nothing can defeat God or stand in the way of His good." God is with you, and He is more powerful than any problem. His Spirit in you gives you the faith to rise up, to press forward, to meet life without fear.

If you were taking a trip by automobile, you would not turn back because of stoplights, "slow" signs, detours, closed roads, tunnels, and so on. Whatever you met along the way might slow you or alter your course, but it would not keep you from pressing forward to where you wanted to go. So in your life there may be things or conditions that seem to stop or slow you, but they are not permanent. They can be met one by one; they need not keep you from going forward.

Are you meeting with a condition of ill health? Do not give in to it, do not give up your belief in health as your heritage from God. Press forward in faith, pray in the sure realization that the life of God is strong within you, that His healing power is active in you. Think of your body as the temple of the living God, alive and aglow with life and light.

If your affairs seem to be in confusion, if there is lack in your life, if the demands made upon you exceed the supply that you have, do not give up, do not despair. Rather, take this as a time of renewal of faith, a time of greater trust in the one Power, the one Source, God within you. Press forward in courage and confidence, taking the steps that God reveals to you as you turn to Him for guidance.

There is always a way out of distress; there is

always a prosperous and happy path open before you; there is always a door opened to you.

Probably our greatest deterrent, the thing that stops us in our efforts, that seems to block our way, is fear. When we are filled with fear, we may feel that it is impossible to meet or cope with the situations in our lives.

How do we overcome fear? Fear disappears as we listen to God's guidance, as we know that He will not fail us nor forsake us, as we know that He is with us, giving us courage.

You surely have had the experience of going ahead with something even though your heart was racing and knees trembling. As you went ahead, as you said to yourself that with God you could do all things, you found that your courageous, decisive action erased fear.

Fear may flash across your mind like a red light. If it does, do not panic; rather, take it as a signal to stop and pray, to let God take over, to trust God for divine direction and guidance.

When a person feels under pressure, he may feel incapable of acting; he may feel that it is impossible to measure up to all that is expected of him, to all that he expects of himself.

No matter how encompassed by the demands of

life you may feel, or how burdened, pressured, or inadequate, the burden can be eased, the sense of pressure lifted, the feeling of inadequacy replaced with a sense of confidence, a feeling of power and ability. When you sincerely seek God in prayer, you are able to let go and let God take over. By letting go and letting God, you open yourself to the power of the Almighty.

To let go and let God does not mean to drift along with whatever comes, good, bad, or indifferent. It means to let go of doubts and fears, of negative beliefs. It means to let the strong, vital, powerful Spirit of God take over in you, spring forth through you.

You are meant to be alive and enthusiastic. You are meant to press forward eagerly. You are meant to grow and unfold spiritually as well as to be whole and perfect mentally and physically. You are meant to know that God is the power in you, the power at work in your affairs, the power at work in the lives of your dear ones, the power at work in the world.

You are at a turning point. Do not give up!

Stand for What You Believe

It is easy to believe in God, to believe in good, when everything is going well; but it is when appearances are negative and distressing that we prove our faith. It is at such times that we find out where we stand and what we stand for.

Do you believe in life, in God's power to heal? Stand for what you believe! Do not give power to disease by believing in it; do not give power to sickness, weakness, or ill health by dwelling on them. Stand in your faith and know that there is only one life, one power, one healing presence: God—God in the midst of you, God in the midst of anyone in need of healing.

What is an affirmation of Truth but a way of standing in faith? Your affirmations of life, of health, of strength, of power are your way of saying, "This is where I stand; this is what I stand for. I believe in God. I have faith in His power to heal."

Do you believe that God's power is greater than any problem, that there is no condition beyond His help, no need that cannot be met in Him? Do not let this belief be shaken when something occurs that seems to pull the rug from under your feet. Stand for what you believe! Affirm that God is in the situation, that His power is there, that nothing can overpower the divine good. If you are faced with some need that seems beyond your capacity to meet or fulfill, now is the time to stand with God, to prove where you stand and what you stand for. Charles Fillmore said, "No one ever went down to defeat who in his hour of need declared the almightiness of God in Christ."

Stand strong, stand fast, declare the truth, declare the almightiness of God in Christ, and you will come through any need, any problem, any situation stronger than ever in faith, filled with the greater assurance of the one Presence, the one Power.

It is easy to love and bless and praise other persons when they are loving and kind and praiseworthy, when they act in ways that are pleasing to us, when we feel that they merit our trust and approval. But where do we stand when someone is difficult, faultfinding, quarrelsome, critical? What is our reaction to those who disappoint us, betray our trust, act dishonorably? If we believe that we are all one in God, if we believe that the Spirit of God, the Christ, is in us and in all persons, then we need to stand for what we believe.

Jesus said: *"You have heard that it was said, 'You shall love your neighbor and hate your enemy.' But I say to you, Love your enemies and pray for those who persecute you, so that you may be sons of your Father who is in heaven; for he makes his sun rise on the evil and on the good, and sends rain on the just and on the unjust."* (Matt. 5:43-45)

What kind of love is this that Jesus teaches? Is it love that condones weakness, that says evil is good? No, it is love that reaches past the outer man, that stands fast in faith in the inner man, the Christ self in all, the kind of love that, though it may not be able to approve of or love what another does, can still love and bless and praise the indwelling Spirit in that one.

Stand for what you believe—about yourself, about others. Do not let go of your vision of the indwelling Christ. Thus is Christ brought forth in the world; thus is Christ reborn in the hearts of all.

Sometimes it seems that when we are trying hardest to live according to Truth, our faith is tested again and again. It is almost as though God were saying to us, "If you believe in me, if you have faith in me, prove it."

All of us long to be of more help to others, to make some real and lasting contribution to the world. Is it not true that the persons who have influenced you most for good, who have helped and inspired you, have been those who stood for what they believed, who stood strong and fast in faith even when the world about them seemed to tremble and shake? You cannot imagine how great your influence can be, how much help you give to others through your attitude of faith and truth, through your sure and quiet conviction that God is all, that God is present, that good is in every situation, in every person, in every condition.

Where do you stand?

You stand in the Truth of God!

Don't Let It Get You Down

Has someone said to you, when you were going through a troubling or distressing experience, "Don't let it get you down"? These words may be trite, but the advice is sound. No matter what happens, no matter how difficult a situation may be, we do not need to be downed by it. We can keep our faith; we can stand steady and strong.

What gets us down? Failure, disappointments, sadness, tragedy? Sometimes, of course. But is it not often true that the day-by-day irritations, the molehills on their way to becoming mountains, are what get us down? Perhaps we are in contact daily with someone who is critical or faultfinding, perhaps a coworker who seems to undermine us and make our way difficult and unhappy. As we lie awake at night thinking about it, we may even see that the situation is more imagined than real, and yet we feel the erosion of the inner irritant, like the shore that is constantly buffeted by the sea.

The most freeing, most uplifting idea you can lay hold of is that there is a Self of you that cannot be cast down, that cannot know resentment or annoyance, that is impervious to the things of the world. This is the Christ in you, the Self of you that is spiritual and free. This is the Self of you that must be lifted up in order that everything in you may rejoice continually and express the qualities of God that are inherent in you.

The lifting up of our thoughts to the Christ is the answer to depression. "Don't let it get you down" is good advice but does not give the clue to the answer.

Let Christ be lifted up in you is the answer. *"And I, when I am lifted up . . . will draw all men to myself."* (John 12:32) *All men* includes the distressed or despairing you. When Christ is lifted up in you, the little self fades into the background; the great and wonderful Self of you shines through.

What we need to remember when we are cast down in spirit, distressed and disturbed by some experience or by some person, is that we do not of ourselves do the lifting up. In fact, we cannot do it. The person who tries to "grin and bear it," the person who vows "I'll be happy if it kills me," usually succeeds only in repressing the unhappy thoughts and feelings, not in getting rid of them.

The Christ in us can be lifted up, not by effort or force of will on our part but by a quiet willingness to be still, to let the Spirit of God flood our being, pour through us, fill us with forgiving love and healing light. It is like struggling with dark thoughts through a long and restless night, and suddenly it is morning and light comes through the windows! We did not bring the light; it is there—and how different everything looks in the morning light!

IX

A Turning Point:
When We Find Inner Peace

Poised, Patient, and Positive

One of the favorite ideas in the Unity teachings is the idea that all things work together for good. It is based on the Bible text, Romans 8:28: *We know that in everything God works for good with those who love him . . . .*

Sometimes it takes great poise to remember this, especially when things seem out of order, when confusion seems to reign in our affairs. Everyone around us may be upset and unhappy, but we can refuse to get down into negation as we affirm: *I am poised, because I know that God is leading me into my highest good, and I know that God is present here, bringing about that which is for the highest good of all.*

Poise is balance. It is, as someone has described

153

it, a <u>combination</u> of <u>peace and power</u>. We are poised when we are peaceful within; <u>we are poised when we feel the power of God within us, at work in us and through us.</u>

I am patient. This is not always easy for some of us to affirm, for we may actually feel very impatient—impatient with ourselves, with our faults and failures. We may feel impatient with others, with those who seem to hold us back, with those who seem to demand our sympathy. We may feel impatient with those who expect us to help them and will not help themselves.

We may feel impatient if we are waiting to hear whether we have been accepted for a job, or perhaps whether our offer on a house has been accepted. We may be impatient if we feel that we are not progressing in our work, or if we find it difficult to keep up with schoolwork. We may be impatient parents or teachers because we expect things of a child that he does not seem to understand, much less come up to.

Affirm: *<u>I am patient because I know that God is leading me into my highest good. I am patient with others, because I know that God is leading them into their highest good. I am patient because I know that God is at work and He cannot fail.</u>*

I am positive. Some people are very positive, but about the wrong things. They are positive that things will never work out. They are positive that someone is trying to take advantage of them. They are positive that someone or something will come to no good end.

When we affirm: *I am positive; I know that God is leading me into my highest good,* we are aligning ourselves with the constructive side of things.

We can be just as positive in our thoughts about others. We can be positive that God is in them, that God is working through them, that God is leading them into their highest good.

We may wonder how the phrase "poised, patient, and positive" applies to healing.

Let us think about poise and healing. True healing is a matter of balance—balance in the body, balance in the mind, balance in the emotions. To affirm: *I am poised; I know that God's healing work is being done in me,* is to affirm perfect balance.

Anyone with a healing need does not question the need of being patient—he needs to be patient with himself, he needs to be patient with those who are trying to help him. He needs to be patient with the healing processes that are at work in him.

I am patient. I know that God's healing work is being done in me. Sometimes healing comes step-by-step, sometimes it is instantaneous. However healing comes, impatience does not hurry it. It may, in fact, stand in the way of healing. Patience keeps us peaceful in mind and heart and helps to free us from tension and anxiety.

I am positive. I know that God's healing work is being done in me. This is a powerful statement, for it embodies a positive outlook, a constructive outlook. It does not say, "I *think* I may be healed." It does not say, "*If* I am healed." It takes a positive stand and invites a positive result.

When we are praying for others, we need to take a positive stand. Our prayer for others can be: *I am positive in my thought about you. I am positive in my prayers for you, for I know that God's healing work is being done in you.*

It is easy to see how these words *poised, patient,* and *positive* have bearing on prosperity. The one who is poised is not fearful about his supply. The one who is patient does not doubt that his good is on its way to him. The one who is positive places his faith in the one true source of all supply—God. He knows that God provides for his every need. With such an attitude, with such an outlook, pros-

perity gravitates toward him. In the face of limitation, he is positive that supply is available; in the
face of delays, he is patient and trusting, in the face
of change, he is poised, knowing that all things are
working together for good.

Let us see ourselves as confident and unafraid,
free from anxiety or doubt. Let us see ourselves as
God sees us, poised, patient, positive, successful,
prosperous, attracting our good to us.

Let these words *poised*, *patient*, and *positive* be
your key words, your key ideas. As you do so, you
will find that everything in relation to your life will
be blessed. You will meet each day knowing that
God is with you to guide you into your highest
good, to heal you of every disease, to provide for
your every need.

How to Be Relaxed, Rested, and Refreshed

Many people find it difficult to relax. They must
keep a tight hold on everything; they must be continually busy; they must prove their worth, their
ability.

It is good to be busy, to be ambitious, to be

eager to grow and improve. But it is how we look at ourselves and what we are doing that makes the difference between frustration and success. The busiest person may feel the most frustrated because he is not satisfied with what he is accomplishing, and certainly the person who will not or cannot let go of any personal responsibility may feel the most tense and strained.

There is a way to relax in the midst of activity; there is a way to live with an easy, happy spirit, so that we do not become nervous or tense.

The very people who say that they do not have time to relax are the ones who need most to learn the secret of relaxation.

Have you ever had a day when you felt so close to God, so at one with Him, that you knew He was working with you in all that you did? Everyone has had such days. And is it not true that they are the days when work seems to sail along, when everything goes smoothly and quickly, when interruptions do not annoy us, when others do not hinder our efforts, when it seems that we accomplish twice as much as we had thought possible?

Such are the times when we are truly relaxed, even though outwardly we are working. True relaxation comes as we let go the feeling of personal responsibility, the feeling that the burden of the whole world rests on our shoulders. We realize that it is God in us who does the work, that we are channels through which His power and love flow.

If you feel tense or tired, if you feel under stress and strain, you know that you should relax. But you probably find it difficult to relax at the time when you most need to, because even when you take time to relax your body, your mind is still racing in circles. The more you try to relax, the more you think of all that needs to be done.

You become tense through trying too hard. You need to learn to let go and let God. Do not try to relax by trying to force yourself to relax. Do not try to make yourself rest; do not try to make yourself quit thinking about all that needs to be done. Do not even think about relaxing, for probably the more you think about it, the more tense you become. Rather, think about God. Start with a simple realization such as: *God is. God is here with me now. God is good. God is the only power. God is all there is.*

God is all there is. Say this over and over to yourself. Lean back on this realization; rest in it. Think of God as surrounding you, enfolding you, upholding you, supporting you.

Rest in God. Relax in God.

> *Thou dost keep him in perfect peace,*
> *whose mind is stayed on thee,*
> *because he trusts in thee.* (Isa. 26:3)

When you find yourself thinking of the work yet to be done, say to yourself: *God is the only power. God is all there is. He does the work.* When you find yourself thinking of persons whose needs or problems have caused you concern, know that God is the only power in their lives, that His Spirit is in them, that He is their light, their guide, their source of strength, their help in every need.

It is important to all of us that we have times for quiet, for prayer, for meditation. Early in the morning, before our day of activity begins, we can set the pattern for our day by thinking about God, by realizing His presence, by giving thanks that we are not alone, that in and through all things God is with us.

Even when we are busy, we can be relaxed in God. We can do our work with such a spirit of inner trust and confidence that we draw continually on the living spring of spiritual power within.

> *They who wait for the Lord shall renew their*
> *strength,*
> *they shall mount up with wings like eagles,*

they shall run and not be weary,
   they shall walk and not faint. (Isa. 40:31)
We can run and not be weary if we wait on the Lord, if in the inner self we are tuned to Spirit, if no matter what we are doing outwardly, we are inwardly resting in the Lord, trusting in Him, living in Him.

Is Your Mind at Peace?

Is your mind at peace? Perhaps you feel that you cannot answer this question unless you are able to say that there are no problems in your life, that everything is as nearly perfect and satisfying as it should be or as you hope it will be.

When you think of the times you have experienced real peace of mind, have there not been times when outwardly there were problems? Perhaps you were as Paul: . . . *afflicted in every way, but not crushed; perplexed, but not driven to despair; persecuted, but not forsaken . . . .* But you had peace of mind, real peace of mind, because you were so filled with the realization of God's presence that you knew, with an unshakable knowing, that God was all and all was well.

Peace of mind is not something you achieve when everything is perfect, when things have been worked out happily; peace of mind is something that often precedes the solving of the problem.

Just as at the eye of the hurricane there is stillness, so in the midst of confusion or distress there is an inner place of stillness, the secret place of the Most High. You can have peace of mind any time—right now—for God's peace is within you. Truly, the only peace you will ever experience is the peace that comes from experiencing God. This peace does not depend on results. Rather, it is the beginning; it produces the results.

James Dillet Freeman said:

Where is the gate to peace?

When you come to it, you will not find a sign saying "Peace."

The sign will say, "Discipline."

The discipline may be renunciation.

It may be work.

It may be courage.

It may be knowledge.

It may be prayer.

It may be love.

It may be losing yourself in search of God . . .

To go through the gate of peace
is to find your right relation
to yourself, to things, and to God.

All things are created in silence. When you turn to God in silence, in prayer, in meditation, when you lose yourself in Him, when you are filled with infinite peace, life does not become passive for you. Rather, life takes on new meaning for you, and the inner peace you have found becomes the gateway to new and greater expressions of the powers and abilities that are yours as a child of God. Work, courage, knowledge, prayer, love—these are peace in action.

Peace and healing go hand in hand. Have you ever thought that if only you could be rid of some distressing physical condition, you would be at peace? It is the other way around: when you are at peace, when you are immersed in the realization that there is only one life, God-life, that you are filled with this life, that there is nothing to fear, then appearances change and peace and healing come forth in your body.

The life of God finds perfect expression in me.
My mind is at peace, and my body is healed.

Think about what this means. The life of God

finds perfect expression in you as you open yourself to it, as you let go of fearful thoughts, as you learn to discipline your feelings, as you keep your mind stayed on God, centered and poised in Him.

The way of prayer is challenging and self-forgetting. It is true that no one can bring us peace but ourselves. But it is also true that only as we forget ourselves and lose ourselves in God do we find peace.

Peace of mind is made up of many feelings, attitudes, actions, and reactions. When you seek peace of mind, you are seeking not blankness, but God in action. Peace is not a stagnant pool to sit beside, but a flowing river, a river of life and energy, of which you are a part.

God bless you, dear friend, with perfect peace, the peace that comes from a disciplined mind, the peace that comes from a will to work, the peace that comes from a courageous approach to life, the peace that comes through knowledge and understanding, the peace that comes through losing yourself in search of God, the peace that comes through finding your right relation to yourself, to other persons, to things, and to God.

The Presence with You

When a person is troubled or concerned about himself or about someone dear to him, often what he needs most is a realization that he is not alone, that the presence of Christ is with him, that even as he prays Christ is saying to him: *". . . lo, I am with you always . . . ."* (Matt. 28:20)

What greater strength can you find than the strength that comes to you when you know that Christ, the presence of life, peace, joy, love, and substance, is ever within, about, before, and beside you? *". . . Your life is hid with Christ in God."* (Col. 3:3)

When you think of yourself as living in the presence of Christ, surrounded by the love of Christ, encompassed by the life of Christ, filled with the joy, the peace, the substance of Christ, the problems that loomed so large in your mind assume their right proportions.

With Christ all things are possible.

With Christ you can do all things.

In Christ you are healed and perfected.

Christ attends you; Christ guards you; Christ inspires you; Christ comforts you; Christ heals you;

Christ prospers you; Christ enlightens you.

Wherever you go, whatever you do, Christ is with you. Christ is in attendance; Christ is the power at hand that you need to meet every situation. Christ is the light that shines into your mind and heart and makes all things clear. Troubled or unhappy thoughts are dissolved in this light; sad or depressed feelings are transformed by this light.

Christ is your life; Christ is the healing power that restores and renews your body; Christ is the life-giving presence in which you live; Christ is the prospering presence by which you are guided.

Christ inspires you to realize your oneness with Him, your oneness with His life, truth, and love.

As you meditate on the Christ, as you think of His presence with you, you come to know that you are one with the Christ, that His power is in you, that His love is in you, that His life is in you, that you have the Mind of Christ.

If you are seeking the answer to some problem, be still and know that Christ is in you, that in Him is the perfect answer to all things, that in Him the way is revealed.

The more you realize and rely on Christ within, the more peace, light, and joy you will experience.

Have faith in Christ to direct your every step, to

relieve you of all anxiety, to cure every disease, to manage all your affairs, to protect and bless you. You cannot expect too much of the Christ. You cannot have more faith than He is able to fulfill, for Christ is all in all. It is when you look to persons alone for help, when you depend on outer power alone to heal you or to free you, that you may be disappointed, let down.

When you turn all things over to the Christ, you find the answers you have been seeking. In following after the Christ, you leave behind the old ways and take on new life, new joy, new power. You are filled with a sense of purpose and direction. The old things are passed away and you become new in Christ.

When you abide in the presence of Christ, you no longer look at yourself or at the world in the same light.

Looking with the eyes of Christ, you see perfection. You see past appearances to the underlying goodness of God. You see past disease to health; you see past poverty to supply; you see past fear to faith; you see past worry and concern to calm confidence.

Listening with the ears of Christ, you no longer hear sounds of discord, hatred, or confusion. You hear the harmony of the universe. You hear the heartbeat of divine love. You hear the voice of praise, the word of Truth.

Loving with the heart of Christ, you no longer harbor resentment or hurt or bitterness. You are filled with compassion, with understanding, with forgiveness. You are filled with the Christ love that sees all persons as God sees them, that penetrates the surface appearances and beholds and loves the perfect child of God that everyone is created to express.

X

A Turning Point: When We Pray

The Prayer of Faith

You are probably familiar with "The Prayer of Faith," for it is one of Unity's best-known and most loved prayers. Perhaps you learned it as a child; perhaps you taught it to your children.

You may wonder why these simple little verses have endured for so many years. From the moment this prayer appeared many years ago, it has had an impact on human hearts and lives. The reason, I am sure, is that it is what the title says it is—a prayer of faith!

There are no words of anxiety in it; there is no note of begging or pleading with God for help; there is no questioning or doubting in it. It is child-like in its simplicity; it is direct; it expresses faith.

How much better it is to hold to the thought,

God is my help in every need, than to cry out, "What will I do? Where can I turn? Where is help to come from?"

God is my help in every need is a prayer of faith. You no doubt have felt consolation in these words many times, as thousands of others have.

When there were difficulties in your life, when you did not know what to do or which way to turn, just reminding yourself, *God is my help in every need,* enabled you to stand strong and resolute.

God is my help in every need. With this assurance in your heart and mind you know that there is no need to be anxious, that with God there is always a way. When you truly and persistently hold to this idea, *God is my help in every need,* His help is revealed.

God does my every hunger feed. We have many kinds of hunger—hunger of the mind and soul, hunger of the body, hunger of the affairs.

If we need more money in order to meet our obligations, if we need employment, if we are wondering how we shall be fed or housed or clothed—God is our supply. *"Your heavenly Father knows that you need them all."*

Even if we have all the outer things necessary to our well-being, we may still have an inner hunger, a soul hunger. We may have feelings of restlessness and dissatisfaction with our lives. *"He has filled the hungry with good things . . . ."* (Luke 1:53)

Our hunger for light, for understanding, for truth, finds fulfillment through the Spirit of God in us. He feeds our inner hunger with living bread.

God walks beside me, guides my way
Through every moment of the day.

To have this sure realization of God's presence with us gives us confidence and inner assurance. We know that because God is with us as wisdom, we will know what to do, we will be able to make right and wise decisions, we will follow in the way that is for our highest good and happiness.

"The Prayer of Faith" is many things to many people. To some, one line will have meaning and this is what they remember when the prayer comes to mind. One of my daughters as a child called "The Prayer of Faith" the "patient, kind, and loving, too" prayer.

When we are emotionally upset, when we have an inharmonious condition in our home or in our place of business, we may wish that other persons were kinder, more loving, more considerate. We may long for peace and love and understanding.

But the prayer-of-faith way is different. It reminds us that harmony begins with us, that peace begins with us. It takes us back to the central idea of ourselves as children of God; it reminds us of our real Self, our divine nature. It says to us: "This is what you are—wise, true, patient, kind, loving." It reminds us of the power that is in us, the Christ.

Through Christ in us we can get along happily with any person; we can cope with any situation; we can express understanding, forgiveness; we can be perfectly poised and at peace. All that we are, can do, and be is possible through the power of Christ in us.

There are persons who do not understand the nature or the effectiveness of affirmative prayer, who ask, "How can you say, 'God is my health, I can't be sick' when you are sick? How can you be heartless enough to send a prayer like this to someone who is ill or suffering?"

When you say for yourself (or, altering the words accordingly, for someone else), "God is my health, I can't be sick," you are saying that which is true in God's sight.

God is the life within us; God is the health of our bodies. If we believe that God is the source of life, then we cannot believe in sickness or disease as lasting or permanent. Everything in us responds to the idea of life; the cells of our bodies wake up and respond to our faith.

Jesus did not qualify His words when He healed. He did not say to anyone, ''You cannot be healed.'' He said: ''. . . *your faith has made you well* . . . .'' (Mark 5:34) He spoke strong, bold words of healing, words of power, words that stirred an instant response in the hearts of those who sought Him out.

God is my all, I know no fear. The prayer of faith is fearless. What is there to fear when we know that we are one with God, that we live and move and have our being in Him?

Many little children say, ''God is my all, I know no fear,'' when they wake in the night. Our children did. It gave them the reassurance they needed, and the bad dream faded away, the fear of the dark left them, and they went peacefully back to sleep.

Wherever you are, whatever you are called on to do, God is with you; there is nothing to fear. Knowing that God is with you, you meet life fearlessly and confidently. You meet life joyously and successfully.

It Is Important to God

Those who say that we should not bother God with trivial matters, who say, "God helps those who help themselves," are right. And so are those who believe that we should pray about everything and anything, large or small, who believe that without prayer we cannot open the way for God to help us.

Prayer is not "bothering" God; it is not expecting God to do everything for us with no effort on our part. When we pray about something, what do we do? We lift our thoughts, we lift our feelings, we take a larger view of things. We rise through prayer out of the petty, limited thoughts and feelings that have bound us to circumstances and problems. In praying, we let go and let God. We let God take over in us. We let God take over in the situations that cause us concern or unhappiness.

True prayer enlarges us, increases our capacity for action, enriches our understanding, enlivens our outlook. When we are trying to solve a problem, God does not write out the solution for us. Prayer quickens our minds and awakens new understanding in us so that we are able to come to right solutions for any and all problems.

If we think that we should not pray about some situation because we do not want even God to know our true feelings, we do not understand either prayer or God. The all-knowing, all-loving presence of God is in the midst of us. There is nothing hidden from Him. He knows us far better than we know ourselves. God is the divine Self of us that is continually seeking expression through us. The more we open ourselves to the light of truth, the more we feel and know our oneness with the divine Power within us, the surer we become of the presence of God with us. How can we withhold anything from God? He is in us, we are in Him! We may think that we are far from him, but at any moment we have but to turn within in faith, believing, and we shall find Him.

The one who prays about anything and everything grows through the experience. The one who tests and proves the power of prayer in some small matter is the one who stands in faith when there are large concerns to be met.

Most of us do very well in meeting emergencies. Sometimes the everyday irritations are what sap our strength and defeat our spirit. So anything that bothers a person, that takes away from his or her peace of mind, is important—important enough to pray about, important enough to look at with spiritual vision, important enough to rise above, so that it can be forgotten.

Some of us may not have big, dramatic answers to prayer, but most of us could recount hundreds of less dramatic and yet unforgettable answers to prayer.

Perhaps our faith was strengthened because of a small incident, not a large one. We prayed, we affirmed Truth in some matter (such as a misunderstanding with a friend), and were astonished at the way things happened to bring about the peace and understanding for which we prayed.

Prayer is a living, daily, constant way of approaching life. It is not something to be used only in life-and-death matters. Neither is prayer similar to making a list beginning, "Dear Santa, I want . . . ." It is holding to God, to the good; it is seeing the divine Presence in all that we do; it is feeling the divine Presence in the place where we are; it is beholding the divine Presence in others.

If it is important to you, it is important to God. To realize this, to pray about that which concerns you, can be a turning point.

Expect Answers to Your Prayers

I believe one of the reasons for the amazing reports of answered prayer that come to Silent Unity is that almost everyone who writes or calls requesting prayers expects something to happen. They expect an answer to their prayer.

What a difference it makes in the way we pray when we pray with expectancy! Our prayers become alive with faith. We pray as if we were in the very presence of God.

Certainly Jesus showed us that prayers are answered, that we should seek expecting to find, that we should ask expecting to receive, that we should knock expecting the door of good to be opened to us.

When you pray to God for guidance, expect it! Expect to be shown the way, expect to have the solution to your problems. Open your mind to His wisdom; expect it and accept it.

With God there is a perfect way out of every trouble; with God there is an answer to every question in the human heart.

When you pray for healing, expect it!

Imagine how the ones who came to Jesus felt

when they asked Him for healing. They prayed with great expectation. Jesus recognized this when He said: *". . . your faith has made you well . . . ."* (Mark 5:34)

Your faith can make *you* well; your expectation can bring you into the presence of the living Christ. You too can feel the healing power of God flowing through you. You too can spring to life again, rejoicing in your healing, praising God and magnifying Him for His miracles of healing.

When you pray for forgiveness, expect it! Expect the cleansing love of Jesus Christ to forgive you, to set you free from mistakes of the past, to erase from your mind the memory of failure, to refresh your mind with newness, to open up a happier way of life and thought to you. When you pray for forgiveness, expect it, accept it. Let your restoration be whole and complete. Let the forgiving love of Jesus Christ permeate and penetrate every part of your being.

When you pray to God for prosperity, expect it! When you pray for prosperity, you are looking to the one Source of all supply. You are placing your faith in the riches of God. You can, you should, expect prosperity, for you are a child of God. Jesus said: *"Or what man of you, if his son asks him for bread, will give him a stone? . . . If you then . . . know how to give good gifts to your children, how much more will your Father who is in heaven give good things to those who ask him!"* (Matt. 7:9-11)

Ask for what you need with faith and expectancy. There is no need too great for God, there is nothing impossible with Him. Always His good is for you, His supply is at hand.

God is your loving, never-failing, all-providing Father.

When you pray to God for light, expect to receive it! *And God said, "Let there be light"; and there was light.* (Gen. 1:3) When you pray for light, God says, "Let there be light." Light streams into your mind, sheds its rays into every part of your consciousness, shines in you and through you, so that even the least cell lights up with a spiritual glow.

When you pray for light, expect it! Expect to see all things more clearly than before. Expect to walk and live in the light.

When you pray to God for strength, expect it! Expect to feel renewed in strength; expect an infilling of energy and vitality; expect to be revitalized and quickened.

God is your strength. He is the strength you

need to meet disappointment or grief. He is the strength you need to overcome belief in weakness or inadequacy. You are strong in the Lord and in the power of His might. You are filled with the strength with which to meet all things, the strength with which to do all things.

When you pray to God for others, expect answers to your prayers, expect God to help and heal and bless those for whom you pray.

"The prayer of a righteous man has great power in its effects." Expect your prayers for others to bring about good effects; expect the power of God to work in and through all persons in a powerful and perfect way. Expect the one who is sick to be healed. Expect the one who is troubled or sorrowful to be given strength, to be renewed in joy. Expect the one in want or lack to be prospered and enriched. Expect the one who is seeking light and guidance to be shown the way. Expect the one who needs freedom from the old life to be liberated and lifted up. When you pray for others, pray in faith, pray expecting your prayers to be answered.

When you pray to God, expect to see changes, expect great and good things to happen. You cannot expect too much of God, for His power to bless is beyond our ability to comprehend.

*"What no eye has seen, nor ear heard,
nor the heart of man conceived,
what God has prepared for those who love
him."* (I Cor. 2:9)

Be Keenly Responsive to Your Good

When we pray, we are filled with God's Spirit. We respond to this infilling of Spirit by acting on it. To sit and meditate and pray and think beautiful thoughts is good, but prayer and meditation should bring us to life, should influence and affect everything in us and about us.

When we are truly aware of the presence of God in the silence of prayer, everything in us responds; the cells of our bodies respond and glow with life and light; the thoughts of our minds are charged with the inspiration of the Holy Spirit; the feelings of our hearts are blessed and transformed by the power of God's love. When we come to God in prayer, each of us may think that we come to Him asking, but we find, as we make ourselves willing and open channels for His Spirit, that we are no longer askers but responders.

Jesus said, as He taught the multitudes: *"He who has ears to hear, let him hear."* (Matt. 11:15) The secret of understanding is the responsiveness of our spirit to God's Spirit. When we become willing and open channels for His Spirit, everything is made clear to us, we hear and see and understand that which we have passed over before. Then we no longer just say words of prayer, we no longer just repeat affirmations of Truth. We go beyond this to responding—responding with our whole being to the Word of God, the living Christ that becomes flesh and dwells among us.

In the thirty-third chapter of Ezekiel, there is a description of the attitude many persons have toward spiritual teachings. The Lord, speaking to Ezekiel, says: *"As for you, son of man, your people who talk together about you by the walls and at the doors of the houses, say to one another, each to his brother, 'Come, and hear what the word is that comes forth from the Lord.' And they come to you . . . and they sit before you as my people, and they hear what you say but they will not do it; for with their lips they show much love, but their heart is set on their gain. And, lo, you are to them like one who sings love songs with a beautiful voice and plays well on an instrument, for they hear what you say, but they will not do it."* (Ezek. 33:30-32)

The people of Ezekiel's day were no different from many people today. People love to hear about spiritual things. They say, "Isn't it wonderful!" and then they go their way and forget about it. There is a difference between real responsiveness to God and Truth and surface effervescence that treats it all as a lovely song, listens to it with enjoyment, even enthusiasm, but dismisses and forgets it.

How can we be more responsive to God, to Truth, to spiritual light and understanding? The more we pray and abide in the presence of God, the more we arouse and call forth our spiritual nature, the more responsive and alive we become.

"Awake, O sleeper . . .

and Christ shall give you light." (Eph. 5:14)

If we feel lethargic or lacking in responsiveness or awareness, we can help to stir up the spirit in us by speaking these words to our minds and bodies.

We have the capacity in us to respond to God and Truth. Everything in us is waiting to answer the voice of God speaking within us. Everything in us is ready to rise up in praise and rejoicing to the Lord of our being.

The faith we have grows as we answer its call in us, as we use it and act on it. The love that God has implanted in our hearts flows freely through us, blessing us, blessing everyone around us as we express the love we feel, as we respond to the prompting of the loving Christ within us.

The hearing ear and the seeing eye,
the Lord has made them both. (Prov. 20:12)

As you think of yourself as keenly responsive to the Holy Spirit, you will discover that He has indeed created in you the hearing ear and the seeing eye. The inner spiritual quickening that takes place in you will open your ears to new words of encouragement, will open your ears to what other persons are truly saying, so that you hear beyond the word to the heart. And where before you may have been blind to many things, now you will see with the eyes of Spirit, you will see through the appearance to the reality and the truth that heretofore have been hidden from you.

Think about this idea of responsiveness. Make it a part of your prayers and affirmations. When you affirm health, for instance, affirm also that you are keenly responsive to God's healing, renewing, restoring power. When you pray for prosperity, give thanks that you are keenly responsive to the prospering Spirit of God. When you pray about anything, pray also for a responsive spirit, a spirit that replies to God's faith in you with a surge of faith and power, a spirit that rises up in response to the promptings of God's Spirit and acts on the truth that is revealed to you.

See How the Fields Are Already White for Harvest

Because all of us think in terms of time, we forget that time, as we think of it, is man-made, that in God there is no time or space or limitation.

Whenever we are able to let go of the time limitation and think in terms of the eternal—the timelessness of God—we make a breakthrough in the spiritual realm, and the healing, the guidance, the help that we seek are there for us.

Jesus said: *"Do you not say, 'There are yet four months, then comes the harvest'? I tell you, lift up your eyes, and see how the fields are already white for harvest."* (John 4:35)

In a sense we are saying, "There are yet four months, then comes the harvest." That is, we look at our needs, we look at the situations in our lives, and we say, "Someday, somehow, things will be better, things will work out; but not now, not yet.''

To lift up our eyes is to lift up our thoughts about time, to lift up our thoughts to God, to look at all things from the standpoint of God's eternal truth. When we look at all things in the light of spiritual understanding, we see not only that there is no time limitation in Spirit, we see more than this: we see that all is already fulfilled in Spirit, that the fields *"are already white for harvest."*

Every time we affirm the truth we are lifting up our eyes; we are proclaiming the fulfillment of that for which we pray.

What do you long for, what do you need, what is your prayer? Have you qualified your prayers with the thought that your prayers may be answered someday, but not now? If you have been praying for health, hoping someday to be healed, lift up your eyes; behold, now is the time of healing. There is no delay, no restriction, no waiting in Spirit. Already is the harvest of health prepared; already is the one life, the one power, the one healing force present within you; already is your healing established in God.

If you have longed for, prayed for peace and harmony and love in your life, are you looking at your environment, at the persons in your life and thinking that it is impossible now to have the kind of life you want, but perhaps someday things will change? Lift up your eyes; the harvest is already before you. The peace, the love, the harmony you long for are ready for you right now. The possibilities you look for in the future are bright and shining in the very moment at hand. The fulfillment of all that you have prayed for is already within you, about you, around you, for you live in God, your environment is God, the persons in your life are part of, one with God. You do not have to wait for everything to change before your prayers can be answered. The change needed is a change of vision on your part. Lift up your eyes!

The answers to all prayers come through us. We are answered by the Spirit in us. Our minds receive answers to prayers in the form of spiritual ideas; our hearts receive answers to our prayers in the form of peace and joy and love.

Nothing is as powerful as a spiritual idea that is held in love and thankfulness of heart. What are spiritual ideas? They are ideas of truth, ideas that come to us from the one Mind, God-Mind.

The spiritual ideas that come to us as we lift up our minds grow and increase in us. And one idea leads to another so that we find ourselves continually enlightened and enriched.

Let your mind dwell on spiritual ideas. You do not create spiritual ideas, you let them unfold in you, and you reap their benefits through expressing and using them.

If you are praying about some specific problem and do not seem to get any light on it, it may be that you have been trying too hard to work it out in the light of your previous knowledge and past experience. You do well to do this, but do not limit yourself or God as to what you have acquired in a few years of living and experience. There is in you yet more than you have ever drawn on or used. Lift up your eyes to the rich harvest of spiritual ideas ready and waiting to come forth.

Place yourself, your problems, your needs lovingly in the care of God, and give thanks that you are right now in the possession of the right idea that is needed to solve your problem. Light and wisdom are yours; even now they are filling your mind and shining through you into all the affairs of your life.

XI

A Turning Point:
Realizing Who You Are

How Do You Evaluate Yourself?

How do you think of yourself? How do you evaluate yourself?

A woman said recently, "I have been told so often, 'You cannot evaluate your own life or progress.' I pray that this is true, for I cannot feel that in my seventy-nine years I have accomplished one single thing, not one, that has proved itself of real or lasting value. Not a happy picture to look on, when one has tried and tried as I feel I have."

Certainly this woman is not looking at a happy picture of herself. More than this, it is not a true picture!

It is difficult for most of us to evaluate our life and progress, and some of us, like this woman, underrate, underevaluate ourselves, and reproach ourselves for failures. We are underevaluating, underrating God as well as ourselves if we think of our life as valueless or worthless, for our life is an expression of God. Every one of us is a unique creation of God, important to Him and to His overall plan of good.

If we cannot think of one single thing of worth we have done, then let us think of the many things that God has done through us.

To live, to breathe, to think, to love—these are miracles enough to justify our existence. They are evidence of God in us, without whose power we are nothing.

Sometimes we look at the creative people of the world—the poets, the artists, the musicians, the writers—and we long to be able somehow to do something as great and wonderful, something as important and worthy.

Jesus did not leave any written record behind Him; on the surface of things there was little to show for His few years of earthly ministry. But what He was, what He lived, what He taught, made such a lasting impression upon His disciples that they whose lives had been transformed carried His message forward to the world.

It may be that the greatest accomplishment of

your life will be an unseen one, but not an unfelt one.

Every effort we make to grow and progress not only has its effect on us but it affects and influences the lives of those about us.

We cannot all be artists, but in our own way each one of us contributes something of value and worth. No one can say that he has not accomplished something of real and lasting value.

None of us has any idea how far-reaching our influence really is, how we have helped and guided, inspired and cheered others, all unconsciously.

Some of us have had the experience of having someone say to us, "I remember what you told me years ago. It gave me the courage to go on." And we do not recall what we said!

There are ways in which we accomplish living and lasting things that are not visible but are no less vital and necessary than the outer works that loom so large and important.

Jesus said: " . . . *For this I was born, and for this I have come into the world, to bear witness to the truth. . . .* " (John 18:37) If ever we wish that we could accomplish some great thing, that we could bring something wonderful to the world, let us remember that this is our cause, our purpose, too, to bear witness to the truth.

To bear witness to the truth is to live so close to God in spirit that our every thought, word, and act is an expression of His Spirit. When we pray in faith, we bear witness to the truth. When we overcome fear, we bear witness to the truth. When we take our stand that God is all and God is good, we bear witness to the truth.

When we realize that we are children of God, that we are made in His image, that we are meant to express His Spirit, we look at ourselves differently. We are not like the man James describes who beholds himself in a mirror . . . *and goes away and at once forgets what he was like.* (James 1:24) We keep always before us the image of God in us, the Christ in us, and we do not, we cannot disparage this image. We know that we cannot fail, that we are children of God. We are children of light and we walk as children of light. We feel worthy and beloved and we feel ourselves growing and expanding spiritually. We bless our lives, past, present, and future, and evaluate ourselves in the light of truth, in the knowledge that we are children of God.

When we pray for illumination, we find that many things are revealed to us about ourselves that we have not known or understood before, for prayer lifts us to a new place of light and understanding.

As you pray, new light will be revealed to you, new truth will be opened to you. If you have disparaged your efforts or doubted your worth, let the light of Christ dispel the shadows and reveal your true self, your God-self to you.

You are an important part of God's creation. You are His beloved child.

The Truth About You

I am going to tell you the Truth about you. How do I know? I know because I know you. You may say, "But you do not really know me. You have never seen me nor talked with me. You do not know what I look like. You know nothing of my background, my family, my friends. How can you know the Truth about me?"

I know you, dear friend, even though I may not know you personally. I know you as a child of God. I know you as a living spirit sent forth from God. I know you as God intends for you to be known. I know you as a spiritual being, ageless, deathless, a part of eternal life.

Will you listen as I tell you the truth about you? I shall not tell you anything you do not already know. I shall only bring to your remembrance things you may have forgotten. I shall only confirm that which you believe in the depths of your heart.

The truth about you is that you were created for life. God breathed His life into you and you became a living, breathing part of life. Your body, which may seem to be material, to be subject to all sorts of distress or disease, is in reality made up of the pure indestructible substance of God. The life of God is in every cell; the power of God is at work in every part; the intelligence of God directs all its activities and functions. Your body is holy because it is the temple of the living God.

God is your life, your strength, and your health. God is in you, the living, loving source of your life and being.

The truth about you is that you have a great capacity for love. You may not feel very loving, and it may seem to you that there are only a few persons who are good enough for you to love or look up to. But such feelings are not the real truth about you. God has given you a heart of love, a heart that does not seek its own, a heart that does not reject or condemn, a heart that is ready to understand, ready to forbear, ready to forgive, ready to rejoice. By the very nature of being, you are a loving person. You know this and I know it, but most important of all, God knows it. He sees you as His beloved child. He sees you blessed,with a loving heart. He knows that you are capable.of expressing great love, for He has created this capability in you. He has made you in His image and likeness, and God is love.

The truth about you is that you are wise. You have understanding, you have intelligence. You may have disparaged your abilities, you may have let yourself believe that you were not as capable as others, that your mind could not retain facts or knowledge, that you did not possess the judgment to act wisely, that you were confused or illogical. But this is not the truth about you. Your mind is one with the Mind of God. All intelligence is within you to draw upon, to use. Your capacities are not limited by what you have or have not learned in the past. Your capacity for wisdom, for knowledge, for enlightenment is as unlimited as God is unlimited.

The truth about you is that you have all the supply you need. This may seem far from the truth as you see it. It may seem that there is lack in your life, that there is not enough money for daily necessities, much less any of the luxuries. But you are one with the Source of all supply, you are one with God, and you live in the midst of a veritable sea of substance. The supply is there. You have but to realize it and to ask in order to call it forth. Supply and demand are equal in Spirit. There is no lack in God; there is only abundance, pressed down, shaken together, running over.

The truth about you is that you are happy. Happiness is not dependent on circumstances, on outer conditions. Happiness is a condition of the heart, and God keeps the spark of happiness, of joy, always burning within you. Even in times of grief or sadness, the joy is there deep within you. It cannot be quenched. You cannot stay down or depressed or sad, for God has given you a spirit of joy, a spirit that finds happiness as its natural state. You are instinctively a happy person, for this is the way God made you.

Yes, I know the truth about you, and I like what I know, for the truth about you is that you are a wonderful person, a living, breathing, healthy, happy, prosperous, wise, loving child of God.

Jesus' Prayer for You

"The glory which thou hast given me I have given to them, that they may be one even as we are one, I in them and thou in me, that they may become perfectly one, so that the world may know that thou hast sent me and hast loved them even as thou hast loved me. Father, I desire that they also, whom thou hast given me, may be with me where I am, to behold my glory which thou hast given me in thy love for me before the foundation of the world. O righteous Father, the world has not known thee, but I have known thee; and these know that thou hast sent me. I made known to them thy name, and I will make it known, that the love with which thou hast loved me may be in them, and I in them." (John 17:22-26)

Read these words from the Gospel according to John. Think about them, not as words of Jesus to His disciples, but as words meant for you, as Jesus' prayer for you.

You may never have thought of these words in this way. To think of them thus will give them new power and meaning. They will become a living, powerful prayer that can transform you and bless and change your life in many ways.

How do you think of yourself? Do you feel inferior, do you feel apart from God, do you long for some sign, some assurance of God's power, of His glory? *"The glory which thou hast given me I have given to them, that they may be one even as we are one . . . ."* This prayer of Jesus affirms your glory; it affirms your oneness, your unity with God. How can you do other than accept this prayer? Christ within you is your glory.

"I in them and thou in me, that they may become perfectly one . . . ." Think of these words of Jesus as a prayer for your perfection in Christ. Christ, the perfect One, has been with you always—this is what "I in them" means. Jesus' prayer for you is that you may know yourself as a child of God, that you may be aware of the living Christ in your midst, that you may be perfected with Him into the image and likeness of God. These words of Jesus are also a prayer of oneness, a realization of the unity of Spirit.

Have you thought that Jesus' words: *"You, therefore, must be perfect, as your heavenly Father is perfect"* (Matt. 5:48) are impossible of fulfillment, at least in the imperfect state in which you now find yourself?

Here then is Jesus' prayer, His affirmation, if you will, for your perfection: *"That they may become perfectly one . . . ."* You can be perfect, you *are* perfect in Spirit, because Christ in you is already perfected, already one with the Father. Christ does not raise you to perfection—Christ is your perfection now. Christ is your glory now.

"Father, I desire that they also, whom thou hast given me, may be with me where I am . . . ."

This prayer is meant for you, these words are spoken to you. The prayer of Jesus is that you may be with Him where He is. To be with Him where He is, is to be with Him in consciousness, to be with Him in a state of faith, of perfect understanding, to be with Him in a state of knowing that there is only God, only good, only His perfect will.

Jesus' prayer for you is that you may know that God loves you. We often think of His greatest message to us as that of love—God's love for us and for all humankind. But His prayer for you is also His prayer for the world and for each person in the world, namely, that each of us may know with all our heart and mind and soul that God loves us.

God loves you with an everlasting love. You are His own.

"O righteous Father, the world has not known

thee, but I have known thee; and these know that thou hast sent me. I made known to them thy name, and I will make it known . . . ."

The name of Christ is the nature of Christ, which can be revealed to us only through faith. Christ is continually making known His name to you. When Jesus asked the disciples: *". . . who do you say that I am?"* (Matt. 16:15) it was Peter who answered from spiritual insight: *"You are the Christ, the Son of the living God."* (Matt. 16:16) The Christ, the Son of the living God, is revealed to us in the silence of our soul. We have had the way prepared for this inner knowing by Jesus' prayer for us to know the name and nature of the Christ as He knew the Christ.

XII

A Turning Point:
Starting Over After Change

You Can Change Your Life

The change we long for always begins with an inner change. Most of us know this, but sometimes we forget it. We forget that our answer is and always will be to change our thought, to turn to God in prayer, to let the freeing, forgiving Spirit of God take over in us and work through us.

It may be that we arrive at this discovery easily. It may be that we see the need for an inner change only after heartbreaking experiences of trying to change the outer, of trying to make other persons conform to our ideas of what they should be or do. When we try to change conditions, things, and persons through personal will, we are disappointed and disturbed. We are disappointed in ourselves and disturbed in our thoughts and feelings.

When we think about the changes we would like to see in our lives, we discover that we are not as concerned about changing things as about changing ourselves. We would like to feel differently about ourselves; we would like to feel different toward others; we would like to feel free from fears and regrets, from hurts and unhappiness.

Even if we wanted to, we could not, with a wave of our hand, change everything. Life is a continuing process, an emerging picture. There is not one of us who cannot look back and see that some experience, from which at the time we prayed to be free, was one of the most helpful and enriching experiences of his or her life.

It is not the experience itself that bound us, it was our limited thought about ourselves, it was our lack of faith in God, it was our own fear and foreboding. Through the experience we drew closer to God, we overcame our fear and made something good and helpful out of what had seemed to be harmful and binding.

If you are unhappy over some condition in your life, if you feel bitter and resentful toward anyone or anything, if you wish that you could be in some other place or with some other person in order to be happy, stop right now and bring your thoughts back to God. Remind yourself that wherever you are, God is there, that the peace you long for is possible to you now in the circumstances in which you find yourself, for this peace is an inward peace that you can achieve even in the midst of confusion. Remind yourself that the changes you long for are really changes in yourself—a change from unhappiness to joy, a change from the feeling of defeat to the feeling of victory, victory through Christ.

Remind yourself that the old things are passed away, that the old you has passed away, that everything in your life, everything in you, has become new in Christ.

Every day, every hour, every moment, you are one with God, and you have within you the power to change and transform your thinking and your life. Nothing remains the same when you pray. Most important of all, *you* do not remain the same, because you see with new faith; you see everything in a new perspective, in its right relation to God.

It Matters Not What May Befall

Probably one of the most important things any of us can know is that there is never a time in life when we are at the mercy of persons or circumstances, that always God in us is greater.

If ever you feel that things are beyond you, that you are unable to cope with the demands of daily living, remember that God in you is greater than anything in the outer. God in you is mighty and powerful; God in you is your strength, your help in every need.

All through the pages of the Bible from beginning to end, this theme of the greatness of God sings its way into the hearts of those who read in faith.

The prophets of old looked to God for help and found that He was with them, their defense and their deliverance. The Psalmist lifted his heart to God in prayer and thanks for God's nearness and unfailing help.

Over and over stories of overcoming are stories of faith, feeling close to God, of assurance of God's power within, ready to help.

So it is with us as we look at our own lives, and

the experiences we have come through, in the light of faith. Although when we were passing through some period that seemed difficult, we may not have been aware of its meaning, now we see how all things have joined together to form the picture that is life; how every part, every experience has had meaning and purpose; how things have worked together for good in ways that we could not have imagined at the time.

Not only is God always with us as our help and strength, He is with us as the Spirit in us that inspires us to reach out, to press forward. He is the Spirit in us that will not let us stay depressed or down, that will not let us give in to the thought of defeat or failure. He is that in us which says, "You can begin again."

The following poem by Frank B. Whitney has been an inspiration and help to me and to many others. I think that you, too, will find these words assuring.

It matters not what may befall,
Beyond all else I hear the call,
   "You can begin again."
My courage rises when I hear
God's voice allay the thought of fear

And when He whispers gently near,
  ''You can begin again.''

When once quite all the world seemed wrong,
Throughout its din I heard His song,
  ''You can begin again.''
An inner joy within me stirred,
I treasured each assuring word,
My heart was lifted when I heard,
  ''You can begin again.''

Begin again? Another chance?
Can even I make an advance?
  ''You can begin again.''
Begin at once by taking heart
And knowing God—of you He's part!
New life to you He will impart!
You can begin again.

If you have let yourself be unhappy or troubled about anything in your life, you can let go of your fear and worry, you can begin again.

You can begin again to trust God, to rely on His ever-present help and power.

You can begin again to look up, to have faith in the goodness of God at work in your life and affairs, in everything that you do.

You can begin again to think of yourself as God's child, created in His image and after His likeness, having His life and health, His wisdom and power strong within you.

It matters not what may befall. You can begin again!

To Rise Again

You have the ability to rise again. It does not matter if everything in you seems to say, "I can't." You *can* rise again!

You have the ability to rise again, for you have the resurrecting Spirit of Christ within you—within your very soul, within your very flesh.

It does not matter how long you have been down; you can rise again. You can be healed. You have the life of God strong within you, no matter how weak you may feel. You are forever one with the life Source; you are never separated even for an instant from God, who is your life, your strength, your health.

You can rise again. Even when it seems that all is

lost, that life holds nothing more of happiness for you, the healing power of God within you is creating a new heart in you, preparing the way for new joys and greater satisfactions. Though your heart may seem downcast, God's Spirit within you is stronger than depression and bids your heart to look up. It keeps you steady; it renews and revives you.

You have the ability to rise again. In God's sight there are no failures. God sees you not as a failure but as a soul learning and growing. It is never too late to change your thought; it is never too late to change your life; it is never too late to rise again. The resurrecting Spirit of Christ is within you, even when you seem to have failed. And even in seeming defeat, the power to rise up is strong within you.

You can rise again! You can rise out of illness, unhappiness, lack of any kind. You can rise out of feelings of sadness or depression. The resurrecting Spirit within you is never sick, never old, never a failure, never poor. The resurrecting Spirit within you is God's Spirit. Feel its power and strength. Feel it lifting up your entire being. You can rise again!

Point of No Return, or Turning Point?

In thinking about the idea of turning points, the titles of two books I once read flashed into my mind. One was entitled "The Turning Point." The other was "Point of No Return."

I believe there can always be a turning point, and I believe that even a point of no return can become a turning point.

We have all had this happen. We came to a place where it seemed as though all our efforts were futile, where some situation or condition looked hopeless—and then something happened, first of all *in us,* whether we realized it or not, and the point of no return became a turning point. The impasse was broken, the condition began to heal, the seemingly irreconcilable differences were overcome. The mantle of grief became a garland of roses; the weight of hurt or unforgiveness was lifted.

Point of no return, or turning point? It's up to us. Not by chance does life take an upward swing, but by choice.

Sometimes we have brought ourselves to what we think of as a point of no return because of fear. We have allowed fear to dominate our thoughts and feelings to the extent that all of life seems a fearsome affair. Everywhere we look there seem to be reasons to be fearful. Even when there is no logical reason for fear, the undercurrent of fear is there. All may seem to be well on the surface, but we are consumed with fearful imaginings. "What if?" "Suppose that?" Fear does not need facts—it only needs the absence of faith, and it makes its inroads into our minds and hearts and lives.

Fear may bring us to a point of no return, but faith turns the point of no return into a turning point.

When or what was the turning point? No one else may have known at the time what was happening in us, but we knew. Like the prodigal son, we came to ourselves. Suddenly, it seemed, we were able to thrust off the shackles of fear. It was almost like coming out of a sound sleep. To the condition, to the fear, to the illness, to whatever it was that had made us despair, had made us feel like giving up, we could say, in effect, "You have no power!" Something in us gave us new strength, said to us, "You can begin again! You can be healed! You can be happy! You can live!"

Sometimes a word we read triggers the turning

point, or it may be the chance remark of a friend. Suddenly we see! We hear!

To look about us in the spring is to be reminded of turning points. Bareness gives way to growth. Life proclaims itself on every side.

> . . . *And my regret*
> *Becomes an April violet,*
> *And buds and blossoms like the rest.*

I read "War and Peace" many years ago, but I have never forgotten one incident in it. Prince Andrei had gone through a long period of grief; he thought of his life as over, of himself as dead to all that mattered. As he traveled through his land in the winter, he passed an old oak tree, bare, gnarled, dead-looking. He thought to himself, "I am like that tree."

It was in the spring when he traveled back across the same route, feeling as old, as tired, as depressed as ever, that he came to the oak tree again. It had come to life—new shoots, new leaves, new growth.

The tree, dead and hopeless, with which he had identified himself, was green and growing and beautiful. It was the turning point for him!

Springtime is a turning point in nature. We too have our springtimes that have nothing to do with the turning of the seasons but with the turning of our thoughts, the upturn in our consciousness, the points of beginning again—the turning points in our lives.

Some of us may look forward to some time in the future as a turning point. The person who says or thinks, "When the children are grown, I will be free from care, my life will be different," is a case in point. Or the one who says, "When my debts are paid, when I have more money, I'll be happy and at peace." Or the one who feels that if he just achieves some longed-for good, some place of importance, he will be free from self-doubt and uncertainty.

But the children grow up, the affairs prosper, the goal is achieved, and in many instances, the same old doubts and fears and feelings of insecurity remain.

The turning point is not in the changing of outer circumstances but in the changing of our feelings about ourselves, the changing of our way of relating to God, to other people, to life.

Life is made up of many turning points. We go through many rebirths in the course of a lifetime. We turn many corners; we take many and diverse paths.

Anyone who has gone through some kind of

severe illness knows how a turning point comes. He may not be fully recovered, but there comes a time when he knows that he is going to be healed. This inner conviction of healing is the turning point.

People have told us that often a telephone call to Silent Unity has been the turning point in healing. The assurance that God was within them as healing life was something they accepted and had faith in. From that moment, they began to get well.

Sometimes people tell us that an affirmation in *DAILY WORD* proved to be the turning point. One woman told how her husband was being prepared for heart surgery. The nurse came to her and asked her to talk to the husband because he seemed so frightened and fearful and did not expect to live through the operation. The woman said that at first she thought she couldn't possibly get hold of herself sufficiently to be of help to him.

She picked up a copy of *DAILY WORD,* which happened to be several months old, opened it at random, and her eyes fell on the words: *You may say it to others as a healing help: Bless your heart. I know your heartbeat is strong and steady for your heart beats with the strength and rhythm of God. God is in your heart. God's wisdom controls it. God's life centers on it. God's love radiates through it, healing and harmonizing it, your body, and the entire world. I give you my blessing. I know that God is blessing your heart with renewed life, and all is well.*

She said that reading these words she felt a surge of renewed faith.

She again turned the pages of *DAILY WORD* at random and read: *In praying for another person's healing, you need feel no sense of burden or anxiety. Your part is to steadfastly, persistently, calmly hold to the truth that the one for whom you are praying is one with God's life. Hold to the truth that God's life fills him through and through. No matter what the appearances may be, no matter what negative verdicts may have been given, hold to the truth that God is ever equal to the healing of any condition of mind and body.*

Tears of gratitude rolled down her cheeks. Others in the waiting room probably assumed she'd had bad news! Then, filled with faith, courage, and joy, she went to her husband and carefully read him the words of blessing.

She says he opened his eyes, jerked off the oxygen mask, demanded to know where she had gotten that, and asked her to read it again!

From that point on, there was never any question

of his recovery. She thinks of the experience as two miracles—her husband's recovery, and the lifting of the burden of guilt and fear of death that had seemed so real to her.

Turning points!

When our children are small, they need us so much that we may find it difficult to face the fact that children must grow up, and in this process grow to be independent of us. Theoretically we know this, but we may not have accepted it. We may feel shut out of our grown-up children's lives. We may feel unneeded and unwanted. We may be unhappy with them and with ourselves and critical in thought, if not in words, of the way they are conducting their lives, rearing their children, and so on.

A woman who had been possessive in her thought about her children and possessive in her love for them said that the turning point came for her one day when she was feeling hurt and resentful because her children did not ask for or want her advice. She said that she prayed to be shown how to help her children, how to set them straight.

These words came to her forcibly, "You are not God!"

A turning point!

She realized that she had been trying to take the place of God in her children's lives, that she had been unwilling to release them to live their own lives, that she had not trusted the Spirit of God in her children. From that point, her relationship with her children changed, because her thought about them changed. Her love became a supportive but freeing love. She saw, too, that she had been trying to hold on to her role that was important when the children were growing up, and that this was the reason for her feeling of loss and emptiness. She had turned another corner and her life needed now to go in a new direction.

What are we hanging on to? Whom are we hanging on to? Our answer may be a turning point.

Turning points need not be (and often are not) dramatic. The man who said, ''Today I walked down the street by myself without fear,'' had passed a turning point. The woman who said that she had been blaming others for inharmony and dissension in her home, and suddenly saw that she was the one who kept things stirred up, had come to a turning point.

Every time we find it in our hearts to forgive and forget some past hurt or slight, it is a turning point. Every time we come through a night of weeping and know that we cannot lose our own, that in God we are forever one with all we love, it is a turning point.

Every time we turn to God in silent prayer and feel His presence and oneness, it is a turning point. We are never quite the same again.

Every time we choose to be a giver rather than a taker, every time we look for something to praise rather than to blame, every time we discard old, limiting beliefs and stand tall and free, it is a turning point.

Point of no return? There is no such thing.

A turning point? It is always there!

And at every turning point, God is there. As we make the turn, God is there. God is with us all the way—through every turning!

About The Author

Martha Smock was editor of *DAILY WORD* for more than thirty years. In that time she helped and comforted millions of people through her writing and her work in Silent Unity.

A native of Kansas City, Missouri, Martha was born in 1913. From birth, Martha was a part of Unity—her mother sent a birth announcement to Myrtle Fillmore, unaware, of course, of the role that Martha would someday play in the Unity movement. Martha began attending Unity Sunday School at age two, was a student of Charles Fillmore, and joined the staff of Unity School of Christianity in her teenage years. She became editor of *DAILY WORD* in 1944.

The magazine was an important part of her life even before becoming editor. She once said, ''I begin each day at home and at Unity with the *DAILY WORD.* Our children and our grandchildren were reared on it. By the end of the month, the copy on the kitchen table is covered with jam and toast crumbs!''

Martha, who was an ordained Unity minister, was a beloved member of the Unity School staff and a popular speaker at retreats and conferences. She also authored the best-selling Unity books *Meet It With Faith, Halfway Up the Mountain,* and *Listen, Beloved . . . .*

Martha made her transition on July 5, 1984.

Printed U.S.A.   134-F-7588-5M-7-85